HOMONYMS
Why English Suffers

by Robert Christman

A HOMONYM
is a word which agrees with another
in pronunciation, but differs from it
in significance, origin,
and, usually, spelling.

BARBED WIRE
PUBLISHING

LAS CRUCES, NEW MEXICO

Published by Barbed Wire Publishing
270 Avenida de Mesilla
Las Cruces, New Mexico 88005 USA

Text fonts Janson Text and ITC Goudy Sans
Cover fonts Impact and ITC Goudy Sans
All illustrations by Christopher M. Kallestad

ISBN 0-9711930-5-3

2   3   4   5   6   7   8   9   0

Table of Contents

This grouping contains words which have the same spelling
and pronunciation, but different definitions.

This grouping contains words which have the same
pronunciation, but different spellings and definitions.

These are words which are spelled the same, but have
different pronunciations and different meanings.

About the Illustrator

Hi, my name is
Cristopher M. Kallestad.
I am 14 years old and have
lived in California all my life.

I love to draw. I have
drawn pictures ever since
I could pick up a pencil.

I like football and
listening to music. I also
enjoy hanging out with my
friends and playing guitar.

I am a Christian and
love my Grandpa with all
my heart. I appreciate the
fact that he let me do this
for him!

*Cris
Kallestad*

About the author

Bob Christman was born and raised in Allentown, Pennsylvania. He received his education at the Sacred Heart Grade School and Central Catholic High School, graduating in 1951. In 1957 Bob migrated to Southern California and worked briefly at KFI Radio before landing a job at KABC-TV in Los Angeles. He is now a retired Associate Director of the American Broadcasting Company (ABC-TV) in Los Angeles. During his career with ABC he helped in the production of many popular television shows including The Lawrence Welk Show, Hollywood Palace, Let's Make a Deal, The Pearl Bailey Show, The Tom Jones Show, The Dating Game, The Newlywed Game, and Password. He also worked on many field remotes during his career with ABC, including the 1984 Los Angeles Summer Olympics, for which he was awarded an Emmy. Bob is a former member of the Directors Guild of America.

Mr. Christman has always been fascinated by word play and word games and this interest clearly shows in this humorous treatment of homonyms.

Bob Christman retired from the hectic world of TV production in 1994. He and his wife of forty-five years, Marie, moved from Burbank, California to Deadwood, South Dakota in 2000 and are "enjoying the hell out of it!" They have four children and seven grandchildren, one of whom, Cristopher, has contributed his illustrations to this book.

Introduction

Those of us who grew up learning the English language had a great advantage over everyone else who attempts to learn English as a foreign language. We had context, the meaning within the syntax of sentences which helped us to understand what many English words mean, even though they sound the same as other words, but have different meanings and are usually spelled differently. They are the dreaded....

HOMONYMS.

From the placement of words within a sentence, we came to naturally understand such sentences as, "Angus is *too* thrifty *to* spend *two* dollars." It is no wonder that homonyms present a major obstacle to the millions of people who confront the English language for the first time, having learned and used another language.

Here is a book which concisely isolates the most common homonyms, explaining their different meanings and spellings, even though they are pronounced the same. While it should prove a useful tool for those acquiring English as a new language, I am also hoping it will be entertaining as well... Life is too short...

This book intends to be a *practical* and *thoughtful* guide, but does *not* attempt *encyclopedic scope* or lofty *academic scholarship*.

To one who masters English homonyms, the rest of the vocabulary is more easily acquired.

NOTE: The words listed herein are described briefly. There may be more meanings (usages) than those listed. Also, there may be more words that could have been included (but that would have stopped you from using your thinking cap). For example; I have a brother-in-law whose name is "Lint" and I wouldn't want his name to be linked with pocket fluff. But overall I think you will get the point—just have fun with what follows.

HOMONYMS "A"

This grouping contains words which have the
same spelling and pronunciation, but different definitions.

ANGLE (1) To fish with hook and line; OR, (2) To try to get
something by using schemes, tricks, or other artful
means; OR, (3) *Mathematics:* - the figure formed by
two lines diverging from a common point.

ARCH (1) A structure forming the curved, pointed, or flat
upper edge of an open space and supporting the
weight above it, as in a bridge or doorway; OR,
(2) *Anatomy:* - the two arched sections of the bony
structure of the foot; OR, (3) The chief, principal, as
in "arch foe."

ARM (1) An upper limb of the human body, connecting
the hand and wrist to the shoulder; OR,
(2) A weapon, especially a firearm; to supply or
equip with a weapon.

ART (1) The conscious production or arrangement of
sounds, colors, forms, movement,or other elements
in a manner that affects the sense of beauty, specifi-
cally the production of the beautiful in a graphic or
plastic medium; OR, (2) A system of principles and
methods employed in the performance of a set of
activities.

ASH (1) The grayish-white to black powdery residue left
when something is burned; OR, (2) Any of the various ornamental or timber trees, or the wood of such
trees, of the genus Fraxinus.

ASS (1) Any of several hoofed mammals resembling and
closely related to the horse, having a smaller build
and longer ears; a donkey; OR, (2) A vain, silly, or
stupid person; OR, (3) *Slang:* - the buttocks.

BANK   (1) A piled up mass, as of snow, dirt, or clouds; OR, (2) A business building in which money is kept for saving or commercial purposes or is invested, loaned or exchanged; OR, (3) A set of similar or matched things arranged in a row.

BAR   (1) To ban, not allow entrance; OR, (2) A popular shape for bath soap products, candy, or gold; OR, (3) A place where alcoholic beverages are dispensed; a tavern.

BARK   (1) A harsh loud voice or the abrupt sound of a dog; OR, (2) The tough outer covering of trees, shrubs and other woody plants; OR, (3) A sailing ship with three to five masts (also Barque).

BASTE   (1) To sew temporarily; OR, (2) To moisten meat periodically with liquid, while cooking.

BAT   (1) *Baseball:* - a stout rounded, often wooden club, wider and heav- ier at the hit- ting end, used to strike the ball; OR, (2) Any of various nocturnal flying mammals of the order Chiroptera, having anatom- ical adaptation for echolocation; OR, (3) To flutter one's eyelashes.

BATTER   (1) A baseball player; OR, (2) A thick, beaten liquid mixture as of flour, milk, and eggs, used in cooking; OR (3) Beat heavily and repeatedly so as to hurt, bruise, or destroy.

BAY (1) A body of water partially enclosed by land; OR, (2) A structure marked off by vertical elements, such as columns; OR, (3) A reddish brown color, or an animal, especially a horse of that color; OR, (4) A deep, prolonged bark, such as the sound made by hounds.

BILL (1) An itemized list or statement of fees or charges; OR, (2) To prepare a statement of charges; OR, (3) The horny part of the jaws of a bird; a beak. (4) A common man's name, short for William.

BIT (1) A small portion, degree, or amount; OR, (2) A pointed, threaded tool used for drilling and boring; OR, (3) Past tense of BITE; OR, (4) A unit of computer information equivalent to a single character of a binary language, i.e. 0 or 1.

BLADE (1) The cutting edge of a sharp weapon or tool; OR, (2) A strand of grass; OR, (3) The tapered edges of an oar or airplane propeller.

BLUBBER (1) To sob noisily; OR, (2) The thick layer of fat of large sea mammals.

BOUND (1) To leap forward or jump; OR, (2) Past tense and past participle of BIND; OR, (3) Headed or intending to go in a specific direction.

BRIDGE (1) A structure spanning a gap or barrier, such as a river or roadway; OR, (2) The bony ridge of the human nose; OR, (3) The replacement for one or several natural teeth.

You may get **DOWN** from a horse, but you can also get **DOWN** from a duck.

BRUSH   (1) Bristles fastened into a handle, used in scrubbing, polishing, or painting; OR, (2) A dense growth of bushes or shrubs; OR, (3) A brief, often hostile or alarming encounter.

CALF   (1) A young cow or bull, or the young of certain other mammals, such as the elephant or the whale; OR, (2) The fleshy muscular back part of the human leg between the knee and ankle.

CAMP   (1) A place where tents, huts, or other temporary shelters are set up, as by soldiers, nomads, or travelers; OR, (2) Something so outrageous, inappropriate, or theatrical as to be considered amusing.

CAN   (1) Past tense of COULD; be able to; OR, (2) A usually cylindrical metal container; OR, (3) *Slang:* jail; toilet or restroom; the human buttocks.

CAPE   (1) A sleeveless outer garment fastened at the throat and worn hanging over the shoulders; OR, (2) A point or head of land projecting into a body of water.

CAPER   (1) A playful leap or hop; OR, (2) A frivolous escapade or prank; OR, (3) *Slang:* an illegal plot or enterprise, especially one involving theft; OR, (4) The flower bud or young berry of a Mediterranean shrub pickled for use as a relish.

CASE   (1) A particular instance or situation; OR, (2) A crate, container or receptacle for holding something.

CERTAIN   (1) Settled, fixed; OR, (2) Sure to come or happen; inevitable, i.e. certain success; OR, (3) Having or showing confidence; OR, (4) Named but not known: "*a certain Ms. Johnson*"; OR, (5) Perceptible; noticeable: "*a certain cozy charm.*"

CHASE   (1) To follow rapidly; pursue; hunt; OR, (2) A groove, furrow.

COB   (1) A male swan; OR, (2) An central core of an ear of corn.

COMB   (1) A tool used to arrange one's hair; OR, (2) To search thoroughly; OR, (3) The fleshy crest on the crown of the head of domestic fowl and other birds.

COUNTER   (1) *Sports:* - a punch given for one received; OR, (2) A level surface over which business is transacted, food is served; OR, (3) To act in opposition to.

COURT   (1) An extent of open ground partially or completely enclosed by walls or buildings: a courtyard; OR, (2) The residence of a sovereign or dignitary; OR, (3) *Law:* - a person or body of persons whose task is to hear and submit a decision on cases of law, or the building, hall, or room in which such cases are heard; OR, (4) *Sports:* - an open, level area marked with appropriate lines, upon which a game, such as tennis, handball, or basketball is played; OR, (5) To try to gain favor of: courting wealth, fame, or love.

CROP   (1) Something that can be harvested, also: the yield of harvest; OR, (2) A group, quantity, or supply appearing at one time; a crop of new ideas; OR, (3) A short haircut; OR, (4) A short whip used in horseback riding, with a loop serving as a lash. Also, the stock of a larger whip; OR, (5) To trim a photograph or other graphic by means of actual cutting or through a computer program.

DARN
(1) To mend by weaving thread or yarn across a gap or hole; OR, (2) *Slang:* - used to express dissatisfaction or annoyance (variation of damn).

DASH
(1) To break, smash, hurl, knock, or thrust with violence; OR, (2) A small amount of an ingredient in a recipe; OR, (3) *Sports:* - a short distance footrace run at top speed from the onset; OR, (4) A punctuation mark used in writing and printing, and in Morse and similar codes.

DATE
(1) Time stated in terms of the day, month, and year; OR, (2) An appointment, especially to go out socially with another person; OR, (3) To determine the age of something, such as a relic, car, or era; OR, (4) The sweet, edible, oblong or oval fruit of the date palm.

DECK
(1) The main platform of a ship; OR, (2) A pack of playing cards; OR, (3) *Slang:* - to knock down; OR, (4) To clothe with finery, adorn: *"We were all decked out for the party."*

S.S. Homonym

DECLINE
(1) To express polite refusal: *"She declined the invitation"*; OR, (2) To slope or bend downward or to deteriorate gradually: *"His grades declined slowly."*

DEED
(1) An act, feat, exploit, or performance in general; OR, (2) A document containing some legal transfer, bargain, or contract.

DIVE
(1) To plunge headfirst into water; OR, (2) To submerge as a submarine or fall through air, nose down, as an airplane; OR, (3) A knockout feigned by prearrangement between prizefighters; OR, (4) *Slang:* -a

disreputable or run-down bar or nightclub; OR, (5) *Sports*: - activities employed to gain short yardage, as in football, or acquire a base, as in baseball.

DOWN   (1) From a higher to a lower physical position; OR, (2) Fine, soft, fluffy feathers of usually young birds; OR, (3) *Sports*: - in football, one of a series of attempts to advance the ball.

DRILL   (1) The tool or its attachment with cutting edges for boring holes in materials; OR, (2) To instruct and exercise by repetition; OR, (3) The training of soldiers in marching and the handling of arms; OR, (4) Durable cotton or linen twill, generally used for work clothes.

DRONE   (1) A male honeybee that is characteristically stingless, performs no work, and produces no honey. Its only function is to mate with the Queen bee; OR, (2) An idle person who lives on the labors of others; OR, (3) An unmanned aircraft operated by remote control; OR, (4) A continuous low dull humming sound (could drive you bonkers).

DUCK   (1) Swimming bird having a broad flat bill, short legs, and webbed feet; OR, (2) To lower or move quickly to evade, avoid, or dodge; OR, (3) To submerge the head or body briefly in water; OR, (4) A durable, closely woven heavy cotton or linen fabric; OR, (5) An amphibious military truck used during World War II.

sound-alikes   **HOMONYM TROUBLE—**
"**Gnat**" King Cole???

EAR
(1) The organ of hearing, responsible for maintaining equilibrium as well as sensing sound; OR, (2) The fruiting spike of a cereal plant, such as corn.

FAN
(1) A rotating device with rigid vanes for creating a current of air or breeze; OR, (2) *Informal,* - an ardent devotee; an enthusiastic follower (from FANATIC).

FAST
(1) Speedy; capable of acting or moving quickly; OR, (2) Accomplishing something in a short time; OR, (3) Firmly fixed or fastened such as with glue; lasting; permanent; OR, (4) The act or practice of abstaining from foods.

FATHOM
(1) A unit of length equal to six feet used especially for measuring the depth of water; OR, (2) To comprehend, understand.

FAWN
(1) To exhibit affection or attempt to please; OR, (2) A young deer; OR, (3) To seek favor or attention; OR, (4) A light grayish brown color.

FELT
(1) A fabric of matted, compressed fibers, sometimes mixed with synthetics; OR, (2) Past tense and past participle of FEEL.

FILE
(1) A cabinet or folder for keeping papers or related data in order; OR, (2) A line of persons, animals or things positioned one behind the other; OR, (3) A steel tool with sharp-edged ridges for smoothing or grinding metallic surfaces.

FIN
(1) A membranous appendage extending from the body of a fish used for propelling, steering, or balancing the body in the water; OR, (2) A similar air-

foil used to stabilize an aircraft, a missile, or a projectile in flight; OR, (3) *Slang*: - a five dollar bill (from old High German fuenf, finf).

FINE
(1) Of superior quality, skill, or appearance; very small in size or weight; OR, (2) A sum of money required to be paid as a penalty for an offense; OR, (3)Okay, as in *"that's fine."*

FIRM
(1) Resistant to applied pressure such as healthy tissue; OR (2) Securely fixed in place, also: determined, resolute, constant, steadfast; OR, (3) A commercial partnership of two or more persons using a name under which they transact business.

FIT
(1) To be the proper size and shape or to measure for the proper size; OR, (2) To be in good physical condition; OR, (3) To be appropriate; OR, (4) *Medicine*: - a seizure or a convulsion, especially one caused by epilepsy.

FLAG
(1) A usually rectangular piece of cloth, of distinctive color and design, used as a symbol, a standard, a signal, or an emblem; OR, (2) To hang limply; droop; decline in vigor or strength.

FLAT
(1) Having a relatively horizontal surface without a slope, tilt, or curvature; OR, (2) Stretched out or lying prone on the ground; OR,

(3) Deflated, as a tire; OR, (4) Lacking qualification, flavor, interest, or excitement; OR, (5) Below the true musical pitch; OR, (6) An apartment on one floor.

FLATTER (1) To complement excessively, to please or gratify, and often done insincerely, to win favor; OR, (2) Having a horizontal surface without a slope, tilt or curvature; more flat.

FLEET (1) A number of warships operating together under one command; OR, (2) Any group of vessels or vehicles owned or operated as a unit; OR, (3) Moving swiftly, rapidly, or nimbly.

FLIGHT (1) The means or motion of traveling through air or space; OR, (2) A number of Air Force planes forming a subdivision of a squadron; OR, (3) An act or an instance of running away, an escape.

FLUSH (1) To turn red, as from fever, embarrassment, or strong emotion; OR, (2) To flow suddenly and abundantly, as from containment; OR, (3) A hand of cards all of the same suit; OR, (4) To cause a bird or birds to take wing suddenly.

FLY (1) To engage in flight by moving through the air; OR, (2) Any of numerous two-winged insects, which includes the housefly.

FOIL (1) To prevent from being successful; confuse as to evade pursuers; OR, (2) A very thin, flexible leaf or sheet of metal; OR, (3) A light fencing sword with a flexible blade tapering to a blunt point.

sound-alikes ABRIDGE – To reduce the length of; condense; cut short. Then there's **A BRIDGE**, which is a structure spanning and providing passage over a gap or barrier, such as a river or a roadway. Not to mention... **A BRIDGE** also, as being the bony ridge of the human nose or the replacement for one or several natural teeth.

FOLD   (1) To lay one part over or against another part; OR, (2) A group of people or institutions bound together by common beliefs and aims; a religious congregation.

FONT   (1) A basin for holding baptismal water in a church; OR, (2) An abundant source of information or news; OR, (3) *Printing*: - a complete set of type of one style.

FORGE   (1) A furnace or hearth where metals are heated or wrought; OR, (2) To give form or shape to metal by heating and hammering; OR, (3) To move ahead steadily but gradually; OR, (4) To make or imitate falsely, especially with intent to defraud.

FOUND   (1) To establish or set up, especially with provisions for continuing existence; OR, (2) Past tense and past participle of FIND.

FOUNDER   (1) To sink below the surface, as to a vessel; OR, (2) To cave in, fail utterly, collapse; OR, (3) One who establishes or formulates the basis for something.

FRET   (1) To become uneasy; vex, worry; OR, (2) Metal ridges on a stringed musical instrument's fingerboard.

FRY   (1) To cook over direct heat in hot oil or fat; OR, (2) A small, especially young, recently hatched fish.

FUSE   (1) A cord or cable that is set afire to ignite an explosive charge; OR, (2) To unite by or as if by melting together; OR, (3) A safety device that protects an electric circuit from excessive current.

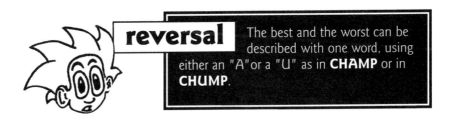

reversal   The best and the worst can be described with one word, using either an "A" or a "U" as in **CHAMP** or in **CHUMP**.

FUZZ   (1) A mass or coating of fine, light fibers, hairs, or particles; OR, (2) *Slang*: - the police.

GAME   (1) An activity providing entertainment or amusement, a pastime; OR, (2) A competitive activity or sport in which players contend with each other according to a set of rules; OR, (3) Wild animals, birds, or fish hunted for food or sport.

GEE   (1) A command for a horse or an ox to turn to the right; OR, (2) Used as a mild expletive as of surprise, enthusiasm, or sympathy; OR, (3) *Slang*: - a thousand dollars - (from the first letter of Grand); OR, (4) *Science*: - the force of one unit of acceleration of gravity.

GIBE   (1) To make taunting, heckling, or jeering remarks; OR, (2) To shift a sail from one side of a vessel to the other while sailing before the wind so as to sail on the opposite tack; OR, (3) *Informal*: - to be in accord, agree: "*Your figures gibe with mine.*" (also Jibe)

GORGE   (1) A deep, narrow passage with steep rocky sides, a ravine; OR, (2) To eat greedily; "*They gorged themselves with candy.*"

GRAFT   (1) To unite a shoot or bud with a growing plant by insertion or by placing in contact with; OR, (2) Unscrupulous use of one's position to derive profit or advantages, extortion.

GRAVE   (1) Requiring serious thought, fraught with danger; OR, (2) Dignified and somber; OR, (3) An excavation for the interment of a corpse.

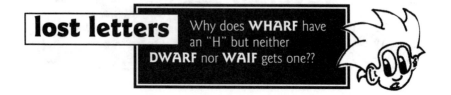

lost letters   Why does **WHARF** have an "H" but neither **DWARF** nor **WAIF** gets one??

GRAZE   (1) To feed, as with livestock, on growing grasses and herbage; OR, (2) To scrape or touch something lightly in passing.

GRILL   (1) To broil on a grill; OR, (2) *Informal*: - to question relentlessly; cross examine; OR, (3) A cooking utensil of parallel bars on which food is grilled.

GRIP   (1) The pressure or strength of a tight hold or grasp; OR, (2) An intellectual, psychological, or emotional hold; OR, (3) A suitcase or valise; OR, (4) A stagehand who helps in shifting scenery.

GUY   (1) *Informal*: - a man, a fellow (guys, refers to friends of either sex); OR, (2) A rope, cord, or cable used to steady, guide, or secure something.

GYROS   (1) Short for gyroscopes or gyrocompasses; OR, (2) A Greek sandwich usually made of sliced roasted lamb, onion, and tomato stuffed in pita bread.

HABIT   (1) A usual manner of behavior; OR, (2) A distinctive dress or garb, especially of a religious order (nuns).

HACK   (1) To cut or chop with repeated and irregular blows; OR, (2) A carriage or hackney (horse) for hire; OR, (3) To work for hire as a writer; OR, (4) *Informal*: - a taxicab.

HAMPER   (1) To prevent the free movement, action, or progress of; OR, (2) A large basket, usually with a cover.

HATCH   (1) An opening (or the cover of same), as on the deck of a ship, on the roof or floor of a building, or in an aircraft; OR, (2) To emerge from or break out of an egg;

how about this...

COINCIDE – Does not mean to go indoors.

HAWK   (1) Any of various birds of prey having a short, hooked bill and strong claws adapted for seizing; OR, (2) To peddle goods aggressively, especially by calling out in the street.

HAZE   (1) Atmospheric moisture, dust, smoke, or vapor that reduces visibility; OR, (2) A partially opaque covering; OR, (3) To persecute with meaningless, difficult, or humiliating tasks.

HIDE   (1) To put or keep out of sight or prevent the disclosure or recognition of; OR, (2) The skin of an animal, especially a large animal.

HIP   (1) The laterally projecting prominence of the pelvis or pelvic region from the waist to the thigh; OR, (2) Keenly aware of, knowledgeable, or interested in current trends or devices.

HOLD   (1) To have and keep in one's grasp or possession; OR, (2) To keep in custody, retain the attention or interest of; OR, (3) The lower interior part of a ship or an airplane in which cargo is stored.

HOOD   (1) A loose pliable covering for the head and neck; OR, (2) The body part over the engine of a motor vehicle; OR, (3) A hoodlum, thug.

HOSE   (1) Stockings, socks; OR, (2) A flexible tube for conveying liquids or gasses under pressure.

HOST	(1) One who receives or entertains guests in a social or official capacity; OR, (2) The emcee or interviewer on a radio or television program; OR, (3) An army, a great number, a multitude; OR, (4) *Ecclesiastical*: - the consecrated bread or wafer of the Eucharist.
HUSKY	(1) Having a hoarse or rough quality, as of a voice; OR, (2) Strongly built, burly; OR, (3) A heavy-coated working dog of the arctic.
JAR	(1) A widemouthed container usually of glass or earthenware; OR, (2) To bump or cause to move, or shake from impact.
JERK	(1) To give a sudden quick thrust, push, pull, or twist; OR, (2) *Slang*: - a dull, stupid, or foolish person; OR, (3) To slice, season, then dry out meat, for jerky.
JUNK	(1) Discarded material, such as glass, rags, paper, or metal that may be reused in some other form; OR, (2) A Chinese flat-bottomed boat.
KEY	(1) A notched and grooved, usually metal implement that is turned to open or close a lock; OR, (2) *Music*: - a tonal system consisting of seven tones in fixed relationship to a tonic; OR, (3) Important, significant, as a key point or player.
KIND	(1) Of a friendly, generous, or warm-hearted nature; OR, (2) A group of individuals or things linked by traits held in common.
KITTY	(1) A cat, especially a kitten; OR, (2) *Games*: - a fund made up of a portion of each pot in a game of poker, a pool of money.

LAP — (1) The front part of the lower trunk and thighs of a seated person; OR, (2) To place or lay (something) so as to partly cover; OR, (3) To ingest (a liquid or food) by lifting it with the tongue; OR, (4) Once around a track or course; twice the length of a swimming pool.

LARK — (1) Any of various birds of the family Alaudidae, especially the skylark, having a sustained, melodious song; OR, (2) A carefree or spirited adventure; a harmless prank.

LASH — (1) To strike or move violently or suddenly; OR, (2) To secure or bind, as with a rope, cord, or chain.

LAST — (1) Being, coming, or placed after all others; OR, (2) To continue in existence or operation; OR, (3) A block or form shaped like a human foot and used in making or repairing shoes.

LAUNCH — (1) To throw or propel with force, hurl; OR, (2) To ready or prepare a boat or projectile such as a rocket, for use; OR, (3) *Nautical*: - a larger ship's run-about boat, a dinghy.

LEAGUE — (1) An association of states, organizations, or individuals for common action, an alliance; OR, (2) *Sports*: - an association of teams or clubs, at a level of competition, that compete among themselves; OR, (3) *Nautical*: - a unit of distance equal to about three miles.

LEAVES — (1) The plural of LEAF, the principal organ of photosynthesis and transpiration in most plants; OR,

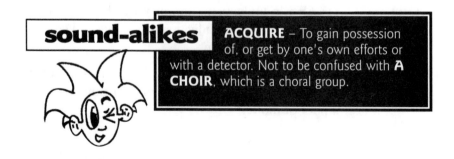

sound-alikes — ACQUIRE – To gain possession of, or get by one's own efforts or with a detector. Not to be confused with **A CHOIR**, which is a choral group.

(2) Goes out or away from: *"He leaves home."*; OR,
(3) Remains, or is a remainder: *"Three minus one leaves two."*

LEECH   (1) Any of various chiefly aquatic bloodsucking or carnivorous annelid worms of the class Hirudinea; OR, (2) One that preys on or clings to another, a parasite.

LEFT   (1) Took leave of location, gone; OR,
(2) Direction, as opposed to right.

LET   (1) To give permission or opportunity to, allow; OR,
(2) *Sports*: - an invalid stroke in tennis and other net games that must be repeated.

LIGHT   (1) Electromagnetic radiation that may be perceived by the human eye; OR, (2) Illumination derived from a source, i.e. a lamp or electric fixture; OR, (3) A way of looking at or considering a matter -aspect; OR, (4) Not heavy, having less force, quantity, intensity, weight, or volume than normal.

LIKE   (1) To find pleasant or attractive, enjoy; OR,
(2) One that is similar to another, counterpart; OR,
(3) *Chiefly Southern U.S.* - to be just on the point of, or come near to.

LIME   (1) A small yellowish green citrus fruit with juicy acid pulp; OR, (2) Any of various mineral and industrial forms of calcium oxide.

LINE   (1) A thin continuous mark, as that made by a pen, pencil, or brush; OR, (2) A system of cables, ropes, string, cord, wire, or pipe; OR, (3) A passenger or cargo transportation system usually over a definite route; OR, (4) A condition of agreement, alignment, trade, occupation, or field of interest; OR, (5) A sequence of related things that leads to a certain ending; OR, (6) To fit a covering to the inside surface, as of a coat.

how about this...

LOAFER – Could be a shoe, a bum or a baker.

LIST
(1) A series of names, words, or other items, written, printed, or imagined one after the other; OR, (2) An inclination to one side, as by a ship.

LITTER
(1) Carelessly discarded refuse such as wastepaper; OR, (2) A stretcher used to carry a sick or injured person; OR, (3) The offspring of an animal at one birth.

LOAF
(1) A shaped mass of bread baked in one piece; OR, (2) To spend time doing nothing.

LOCK
(1) A device operated by a key, combination, or key-card and used, as on a door, for holding, closing, or securing; OR, (2) Sections of a waterway linking large bodies of water; OR, (3) A length or curl of hair, a tress.

LODGE
(1) A cottage or cabin used as a temporary abode or shelter; OR, (2) Native American dwelling, such as a hogan, wigwam, or longhouse; OR, (3) The meeting hall and local chapter of certain fraternal organizations; OR, (4) To register a charge or complaint before an authority.

LOG
(1) A usually large section of a fallen or felled tree; OR, (2) The record, or the book in which the record is kept, of a vehicle's (land, sea, or air) performance OR, (3) To travel; distance or speed, and to spend or accumulate time.

LONG
(1) Extending a relatively great distance or duration; OR, (2) To have an earnest, heartfelt desire, especially for something beyond reach.

LOOM — (1) To come into view as a massive, distorted, or indistinct image; OR, (2) An apparatus for weaving together threads or yarns into cloth.

LUMBER — (1) Timber sawed into boards, planks, or other structural members of standard or specified length; OR, (2) To walk or move heavily or clumsily.

LUSH — (1) Having or covered with abundant growth; OR, (2) A habitual heavy drinker.

MARCH — (1) The third month of the year in the Gregorian calendar; OR, (2) To walk or cause to walk steadily and rhythmically forward and in step with others; OR, (3) A musical composition with rhythm suitable for marching.

MAROON — (1) To put ashore on a deserted island or coast and intentionally abandon; OR, (2)A dark reddish-blue color.

MATCH — (1) One that is like another in one or more specified qualifiers; OR, (2) *Sports*: - a game or contest between two or more individuals; OR, (3) A narrow piece of wood or cardboard, coated on one end with a compound that ignites through friction.

MAY — (1) Is allowed or permitted to; OR, (2) Used to indicate a certain measure of likelihood or possibility; OR, (3) The fifth month of the year in the Gregorian calendar.

 **lost letters** Taking the **OOZ** sound from **DUES** would make the day after Monday, **TOOZDAY**!

daffy-nitions A **HUMMINGBIRD** – A bird who doesn't know the lyrics.

MEAL   (1) The edible whole or coarsely ground grains of a cereal; OR, (2) The food served and eaten at a customary time or occasion.

MEAN   (1) To define, intend, convey, indicate, symbolize, signify, or represent; OR, (2) Cruel, spiteful, petty, or miserly; OR, (3) Midway between extremes, the number in a population that occurs most frequently.

MELD   (1) To declare a combination of cards for inclusion in one's score in various card games, such as pinochle; OR, (2) To cause to merge or become blended.

METER   (1) The measured arrangement of words in poetry, as by accentual rhythm, syllabic quantity, or the number of syllables in a line; OR, (2) *Music:* - the division into measures or bars of specific rhythms; OR, (3) The basic metric unit of length, approximately equal to 39.37 inches; OR, (4) Any of various devices designed to measure time, speed, distance, intensity, volume, or to regulate.

MINE   (1) The site of excavation in the earth, with its surface buildings, shafts, and equipment, from which ore or minerals can be extracted; OR, (2) Used to indicate that which belongs to me.

MINT   (1) A place where coins are manufactured by authority of a government; OR, (2) Various plants of the genus Mentha, having aromatic foliage and cultivated for their oil, used for flavor or aroma; OR, (3) A candy flavored with said plant's oil.

MISS	(1) To fail to hit, reach, catch, meet, or make contact with; OR, (2) To fail to perceive, understand, achieve, attain, attend or perform; OR, (3) A young woman or girl, or courteous title for same.
MOLD	(1) A hollow form or matrix made of plastic, steel, or clay used for shaping fluid or molten substances; OR, (2) Any of various fungi that often cause disintegration of organic matter.
MOLE	(1) A small congenital growth on the human skin, slightly raised and dark; OR, (2) Any of various small mammals usually living underground having strong forefeet for burrowing; OR, (3) A spy who operates as a double agent from within an organization.
MUFF	(1) To perform or handle clumsily: a bungling performance; OR, (2) *Sports*: - to fail to make a comparatively easy play; OR, (3) A small fur or cloth tube in which the hands are placed for warmth.
MUG	(1) A heavy cylindrical drinking cup usually having a handle; OR, (2) *Informal*: - the human face; OR, (3) To threaten or assault (a person) with the intent to rob.
MULE	(1) A hybrid offspring of a male donkey and a female horse; OR, (2) *Slang*: - a person who serves as a courier of illegal drugs; OR, (3) A slipper that has no counter or strap to fit around the heel.
MUSH	(1) Cereal or porridge that is thick, soft, and pulpy such as cornmeal boiled in water or milk; OR, (2) To travel especially over snow with a sled drawn by dogs.
MUZZLE	(1) The forward, projecting part of the head of certain animals, such as dogs; OR, (2) A leather device, fitted over an animal's snout, to prevent biting, barking or eating; OR, (3) The forward, discharging end of the barrel of a firearm.

NAG   (1) To annoy by constant scolding, complaining or urging; OR, (2) A horse, especially an old or worn-out horse.

NAIL   (1) A slim, pointed piece of metal hammered into material as a fastener; OR, (2) Fingernail, toenail, claw, or talon; OR, (3) To capture, to get right: *"He nailed the test."*

NAP   (1) A brief sleep, often during the day; OR, (2) A soft or downy fibrous surface on yarn and cloth; OR, (3) The soft hair on an animal.

NET   (1) A meshed fabric twisted, knotted, or woven together at regular intervals; OR, (2) *Business*: - remaining amount after all deductions have been made; OR, (3) *Sports*: - the woven rope used as an extension of the goal (basketball); the woven rope used at the center of the court (tennis).

NIP   (1) To seize, bite, remove, or sever by pinching or snipping; OR, (2) A very small amount of liquor.

NOODLE   (1) A narrow, ribbon-like strip of dried dough; OR, (2) *Slang*: - the human head; OR, (3) *Music*: - to improvise music on an instrument in an idle, haphazard fashion.

NOVEL   (1) A fictional prose narrative of considerable length; OR, (2) Strikingly new, unusual, or different.

OOZE   (1) To flow or leak out slowly through small openings; OR, (2) A soft deposit (as of mud) on the bottom of a body of water.

OPERATE   (1) To perform a function, such as surgery; OR,
(2) To run, as heavy equipment.

ORGAN   (1) A musical instrument having sets of pipes sounded by compressed air and controlled by keyboards; OR, (2) *Biology*: - a differentiated part of an organism, such as an eye, a wing, or a leaf, that performs a specific function.

OWN   (1) Of or belonging to oneself, to have or possess; OR, (2) To admit or acknowledge, such as confessing, own up to.

PAD   (1) A cushion-like mass of soft material to protect against jarring, scraping, or injury; OR, (2) An ink-soaked cushion used to ink a rubber stamp; OR, (3) A number of stacked, sized, sheets of paper glued together at one end; OR, (4) The cushion-like flesh under the toes and feet of many animals; OR, (5) To line or stuff with soft material; OR, (6) To lengthen (written or spoken) with extraneous material; OR, (7) *Slang*: - one's apartment or room.

PADDLE   (1) *Nautical*: - a wooden implement having a blade at one end used without an oarlock to propel a canoe or small boat; OR, (2) *Sports*: - a light wooden racket used in playing table tennis; OR, (3) To spank as a punishment.

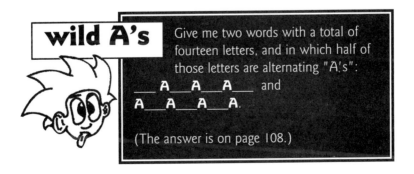

wild A's   Give me two words with a total of fourteen letters, and in which half of those letters are alternating "A's":

___ A__ A__ A__ and
A__ A__ A__ A.

(The answer is on page 108.)

PAGE
(1) A single leaf (as of a book, letter, or manuscript); OR, (2) A youth in attendance at court; OR, (3) A person employed to carry messages or act as a guide; OR, (4) To summon by repeatedly calling out the name of.

PALM
(1) Any of various chiefly tropical evergreen trees, shrubs, or woody vines having unbranched stems topped by a crown of large pinnate or palmate leaves; OR, (2) The inner surface of the hand, from the wrist to the base of the fingers.

PAN
(1) A shallow, wide, open container, usually of metal, used for many domestic and industrial purposes; OR, (2) *Informal*: - to criticize or review harshly; OR, (3) To turn out well, be successful: *"The new business really panned out."*; OR, (4) To move a movie or TV camera to create a panoramic effect.

PANHANDLE
(1) A narrow strip of territory projecting from a larger, broader area, as in Alaska, Florida, Idaho, Oklahoma, Texas, and West Virginia; OR, (2) To approach strangers and beg for money or food; OR, (3) The handle of a pan.

PAT
(1) To stroke lightly as a gesture of affection; OR, (2) Exactly suited to the occasion.

PAW
(1) The clawed foot of a quadruped animal; OR, (2) *Slang*: - the human hand; OR, (3) To feel or handle clumsily, rudely, or with too much familiarity.

PAWN
(1) Something given as security for a loan, a pledge or guarantee; OR, (2) A person or an entity used to further the purposes of another; OR, (3) *Games*: - a chess piece of the least value.

PECK
(1) A measurement, approximately 8 quarts; OR, (2) A quick kiss; OR, (3) To strike or pierce with a beak or a pointed instrument.

peep

PEEP (1) To peer slyly through an aperture or from behind something; OR, (2) The short, soft, high pitched sounds of a baby bird.

PELT   (1) The skin of a fur-bearing animal; OR, (2) To strike or assail repeatedly with blows or missiles, to bombard.

PEN   (1) An instrument for writing or drawing with ink; OR, (2) Any of various enclosures used for animals; OR, (3) *Informal*: - a penitentiary, a prison.

PERCH   (1) A rod or branch serving as a roost for a bird; OR, (2) Any of various spiny-finned freshwater fishes of the genus Perca.

PERK   (1) To cause to stick up quickly, as a dog's ears; OR, (2) An incentive in addition to wages; OR, (3) *Informal*: - short for 'percolate'.

PICK   (1) To select, gather, choose from a group; OR, (2) A tool consisting of a curved bar sharpened at both ends and fitted to a long handle.

PIKE   (1) A freshwater game and food fish that has a long snout and attains a length of over four feet; OR, (2) A superhighway, a turnpike.

PILE   (1) A quantity of objects stacked or thrown together in a heap; to create such a heap; OR, (2) A heavy beam driven into the earth as a support for a structure.

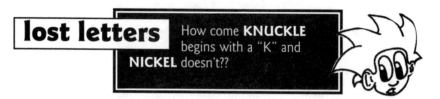

lost letters How come **KNUCKLE** begins with a "K" and **NICKEL** doesn't??

PINE
(1) Any of various evergreen trees, or the wood of such trees, of the genus Pinus; OR, (2) To wither or waste away from longing or grief.

PIT
(1) A natural or artificial hole or cavity in the ground; OR, (2) *Sports*: - an area beside a racecourse where cars are refueled or serviced; OR, (3) An often sunken area designed for a particular use, as that in an arena, a symphony hall, or an amphitheater; OR, (4) The gambling area of a casino; OR, (5) The single kernel or stone of certain fruits, such as a peach or cherry.

PITCH
(1) Any of various thick, dark sticky substances obtained from the distillation residue of coal tar, wood tar, or petroleum and used for waterproofing, roofing, caulking, and paving; OR, (2) *Baseball*: - to throw from the mound to the batter; OR, (3) To erect or establish, to set up, as a tent; OR, (4) *Music*: - highness or lowness of sound; OR, (5) The angle of anything - up or down; OR, (6) To make a case for.

PITCHER
(1) *Baseball*: - the player who throws the ball from the mound to the batter; OR, (2) A container for liquids, usually having a handle and a lip or spout for pouring.

PLAQUE
(1) A small ornament or badge of membership; OR, (2) A deposit that builds up on teeth, or the inner lining of a blood vessel; OR, (3) An ornamental or engraved plate, slab, or disk used for decoration, or on a monument for information.

POACH
(1) To cook in a boiling or simmering liquid; OR, (2) To hunt or fish unlawfully.

POD — (1) A dry, several-seeded, dehiscent fruit, such as the pea; OR, (2) *Aerospace*: - a detachable compartment on a spacecraft for carrying personnel or instrumentation; OR, (3) A group of marine mammals, such as seals, whales, or dolphins.

POKER — (1) A metal rod used to stir a fire; OR, (2) *Games*: - various card games played by two or more players who bet on the value of their hands.

POLICY — (1) A course of action, guiding principle, or procedure considered expedient, prudent, or advantageous; OR, (2) A written contract or certificate of insurance.

POOL — (1) A body of still water at ground level or below ground; OR, (2) *Games*: - any of several games played on a six pocket billiard table; OR, (3) *Games*: - the common fund of money that is later paid to the winner, such as in a lottery; OR, (4) A grouping of resources for the common advantage of participants.

POOP — (1) A superstructure at the stern of a ship, a poop deck; OR, (2) *Slang*: - to cause or become fatigued, tire; OR, (3) *Slang*: - inside information; OR, (4) *Slang*: - a disagreeable person, (short for nincompoop); OR, (5) Excrement, to defecate.

POP — (1) To make a short, sharp, explosive sound; OR, (2) *Baseball*: - to hit a short high fly ball to an infielder; OR, (3) *Informal*: - father; OR, (4) *Informal*: - of or for the general public; pop art, pop music (from POPULAR); OR, (5) *Slang*: - reference to carbonated soda.

sound-alikes SYNTAX – The study of the rules whereby words or other elements of sentence structure are combined to form grammatical sentences. But we also have (informally) **SIN TAX**, a tax on certain items such as cigarettes and alcohol, that are regarded as neither necessities nor luxuries.

PORT   (1) A place on a waterway with facilities for loading and unloading ships; OR, (2) *Computers*: - a connection point for a peripheral device; OR, (3) The left hand side of a ship or aircraft, as one faces forward; OR, (4) A hole in an armored vehicle or fortified structure for viewing or firing; OR, (5) A rich sweet fortified wine; OR, (6) To carry (a weapon) diagonally across the body, with the muzzle or blade near the left shoulder.

POSE   (1) To assume or hold a particular position or posture; OR, (2) To represent oneself falsely, to pretend; to puzzle, confuse, or baffle.

POST   (1) A long piece of wood or other material set upright into the ground to serve as a marker or support; OR, (2) *Sports*: - a goal post; a starting post; OR, (3) A battery terminal; OR, (4) An earring's short bar that passes through the ear and fits into a cap; OR, (5) The grounds and buildings of a military base; OR, (6) A position of employment, especially an appointed public office; OR, (7) To mail a letter; OR, (8) To affix to a usual place for public notices; OR, (9) To enter in a ledger.

POT   (1) Any of various domestic containers made of pottery, metal, or glass; OR, (2) *Slang*: - Marijuana.

POUND   (1) A unit of weight equal to 16 ounces; OR, (2) To strike repeatedly and forcefully; OR, (3) A public enclosure for the confinement of stray dogs or livestock; OR, (4) British currency – the pound sterling.

how about this...

If an **ODE** is a lyric poem, could you call the poet an **ODER**?

PRAYER   (1) A reverent petition to a god, or another object of worship; OR, (2) One who prays.

PRIMER   (1) An elementary textbook for teaching children to read; OR, (2) A device for igniting an explosive; OR, (3) An undercoat of paint.

PROMPT   (1) On time; punctual, done without delay; OR, (2) A reminder; OR, (3) To give rise to, inspire, as a cue in theatrical performances.

PROP   (1) An object placed beneath or against a structure to keep it from falling or shaking, a support; OR, (2) A theatrical property; OR, (3) *Informal*: - a propeller.

PRY   (1) To look or inquire closely, curiously, or inquisitively; OR, (2) To raise, move or force open with a lever.

PUG   (1) A small sturdy dog originating in China, having a snub nose, a wrinkled face, a squarish body, short hair, and a curled tail; OR, (2) *Slang*: - a fighter, especially a boxer.

PUMP   (1) A machine or device for raising, compressing or transferring fluids; OR, (2) A woman's shoe that has medium or high heels and no fastenings.

PUNCH   (1) A tool for forcing a pin, bolt or rivet in or out of a hole, or for circular or other piercing; OR, (2) To hit with a sharp blow of the fist; OR, (3) A beverage of fruit juices and carbonated water or soda.

PUNT   (1) *Football*: - to kick the ball dropped from the hands before it touches the ground; OR, (2) The indention in the bottom of a champagne or wine bottle.

PUPIL   (1) A student under the direct supervision of a teacher or professor; OR, (2) The apparently black circular opening in the center of the iris of the eye.

PUTTER (1) *Sports*:- a short golf club used for putting; OR,
(2) To move or act aimlessly or idly.

QUACK (1) The characteristic sound made by a duck; OR,
(2) An untrained person who pretends to be a physician.

QUARRY (1) Hunted animals; game; OR, (2) An open excavation or pit from which various materials are mined.

QUIVER (1) To shake with a slight trembling motion; OR,
(2) An archer's portable case for holding arrows.

RACE (1) A human population distinguished as a more or less distinct group by genetically transmitted physical characteristics; OR, (2) *Sports*: - a competition of speed, as in running or riding.

RACK (1) A framework or stand in or on which to hold, hang, or display various articles; OR, (2) An instrument of torture on which a body is stretched; OR, (3) A rib cut of meat, from between the shoulders and the loin; OR, (4) *Games*: - a triangular frame for arranging billiard balls at the start of a game, or arranging balls in that frame.

RACKET (1) A loud distressing noise; OR, (2) *Sports:* - (also RACQUET) an oval frame with a tightly interlaced network of strings and a handle, used in various games; OR, (3) *Slang:* - a dishonest enterprise that obtains money through fraud.

RAFT (1) A flat floatable structure, typically made of planks, logs, or barrels; OR, (2) A great number, amount, or collection.

lost letters As confusing as **WATT** and **WHAT** may be, how do you account for **YACHT**??

reversal | **NATION** – A country. Change the "A" to an "O" and you have **NOTION**. What an idea.

RAG (1) A scrap of cloth used for cleaning, washing, or dusting; OR, (2) *Slang:* - to tease, taunt, berate, or scold; OR, (3) *Music:* - a composition in ragtime.

RAP (1) To hit sharply and swiftly; to strike; OR, (2) Responsibility for or consequences of an action; OR, (3)*Slang:* - a talk, conversation, or discussion; OR, (4) *Music:* - a form of popular music characterized by spoken or chanted rhyming lyrics with a syncopated, repetitive, rhythmic accompaniment.

RARE (1) Infrequently occurring; uncommon; thin in density; OR, (2) Cooked for a short time to retain juice and redness.

RASH (1) Characterized by or resulting from ill-considered haste or boldness; OR, (2) An outbreak of many instances within a brief period; OR, (3) An outbreak or eruption on the skin.

REAM (1) A prepackaged quantity of paper dependent on weight, usually 500 sheets; OR, (2) To form, shape, taper, or enlarge (a hole) with a reamer.

REAR (1) The point or area behind the center point; OR, (2) *Informal:* - the buttocks; the hind part; OR, (3) To care for (a child or children) during the early stages of life; bring up.

REEL (1) A device that turns on an axis and is used for winding and storing rope, tape, film, or other flexible material; OR, (2) To be thrown or fall off balance; to stagger, lurch, or sway; OR, (3) A music and its accompanying fast dance of Scottish origin.

REFRAIN   (1) To hold oneself back; forbear; restrain; OR,
(2) A phrase or verse repeated at intervals through-
out a song or poem.

RETAINER   (1) One that retains, as a device, frame, or groove
that restrains or guides; OR, (2) *Dentistry:* - an appli-
ance used to hold teeth in a fixed position; OR,
(3) The fee paid to and/or a professional adviser,
such as an attorney.

RIDDLE   (1) To pierce with numerous holes; to perforate; OR,
(2) A question or statement requiring thought to
answer or understand; a conundrum.

RIFLE   (1) A firearm with a rifled (spiral grooved) bore, designed to be fired from the shoulder; OR, (2) To search
with intent to steal; to ransack, plunder, or pillage.

RINGER   (1) *Games:* - a horseshoe or quoit thrown so as to
encircle the peg; OR, (2) One that rings, especially
one that sounds a bell or chime; OR, (3) *Slang:* - a
(usually superior) contestant entered dishonestly into
a competition; OR, (4) *Slang:* - one who bears a
striking resemblance to another.

ROCK   (1) Relatively hard, naturally formed mineral or petri-
fied matter; stone; OR, (2) To move back and forth,
or from side to side rhythmically; OR, (3) *Music:* -
short description of rock 'n' roll; OR, (4) *Slang:* - a
large gem, especially a diamond.

ROCKY   (1) Consisting of, containing, or abounding in rock
or rocks; OR, (2) Inclined or prone to totter;
unsteady; discouraging or disappointing.

RUBBER   (1) A yellowish, amorphous, elastic material obtained
from the milky sap of various tropical plants; OR, (2)
The final or odd game played to declare a winner or
break a tie; OR, (3) *Slang:* - referring to a thin flexible
sheath made of thin rubber or latex, designed to cover
the penis during sexual intercourse for contraceptive

purposes or as a means of preventing sexually transmitted diseases.

RULER   (1) One, such as a monarch or dictator, who rules or governs; OR, (2) A straightedge strip, as of wood or metal, for drawing straight lines and measuring lengths.

RUNG   (1) A rod, bar, or crosspiece forming a step or a brace, as on a ladder; OR, (2) The past participle of RING.

RUT   (1) A sunken track or groove made by the passage of vehicles; OR, (2) The annually recurring period of sexual excitement in male deer; OR, (3) A fixed routine.

SACK   (1) A large bag of various strong materials for holding objects in bulk; OR, (2) To loot or pillage a captured city or town; OR, (3) *Informal:* - a bed, mattress, or sleeping bag; OR, (4) *Slang:* - to dismiss from employment; OR, (5) *Baseball:* - a base; *Football,* - to tackle a quarterback behind the line.

SAGE   (1) One venerated for experience, judgement, and wisdom; OR, (2) Any of various plants whose leaves are used as a cooking herb.

SAP   (1) The essential fluid contents of a plant; OR, (2) To deplete or weaken gradually, devitalize; OR, (3) *Slang:* - a gullible person; a dupe.

SASH   (1) A band or ribbon worn about the waist as ornament, or over the shoulder as a symbol of rank; OR, (2) A frame in which the panes of a window or door are set.

SAW   (1) Any of various tools, either manual or powered, having a thin metal blade with a sharp toothed edge used for cutting wood, metal or other material; OR, (2) A familiar saying, especially one that has become trite through repetition; OR, (3) The past tense of SEE.

SCAB   (1) A crust discharged from and covering a healing wound; OR, (2) An employee who works while others are on strike, or a person hired to replace a striking worker.

SCALE   (1) Piece of plate-like dermal or epidermal structures that form the external covering of fishes, reptiles, and certain mammals; OR, (2) A mineral coating that forms on the inside surface of various containers in which water is repeatedly heated; OR, (3) A standard of measurement or judgement; a criterion; OR, (4) *Music:* - an ascending or descending series of tones varying in pitch, arrangement and interval size; OR, (5) To climb up or over; ascend; OR, (6) An instrument or a machine used for weighing.

SCORE   (1) Marks made to keep a tally; OR, (2) *Sports:* - a usually numerical record indicative of who is winning or losing a competitive event; OR, (3) A result, usually expressed numerically, of a test or examination; OR, (4) A group of 20 items; OR, (5) A grievance that is harbored and requires satisfaction: "*Settle an old score*"; OR, (6) *Music:* - the written form of a composition for orchestral of vocal parts either complete or for a par-

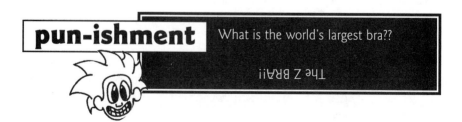

pun-ishment   What is the world's largest bra??

The Z BRA!!

ticular instrument or voice; OR, (7) *Slang:* - the act of buying illicit drugs; a successful robbery; a sexual conquest; securing an advantage: "*The big score.*"

SCOUR   (1) To clean, polish, or wash away by scrubbing vigorously; OR, (2) To search through or over thoroughly.

SCOUT   (1) To spy on or explore carefully in order to obtain information, reconnoiter; OR, (2) One who is employed to discover and recruit talented persons, especially in the fields of sports and entertainment; OR, (3) A member of the Boy Scouts or Girl Scouts; OR, (4) The name of Tonto's horse.

SCRAP   (1) A small piece or bit; a fragment; OR, (2) Discarded waste material, especially metal suitable for reprocessing; OR, (3) To scuffle or fight, often with the fists.

SCRIPT   (1) Handwriting, or a style of writing with cursive characters; OR, (2) The text of a play, broadcast, or movie, or a copy of the text used by the director or performer.

SCRUB   (1) To remove dirt, stains, or impurities either chemically or by hard rubbing; OR, (2) *Slang:* - to cancel or abandon, as a space mission; drop; OR, (3) To wash the hands thoroughly, as before performing surgery; OR, (4) A straggly, stunted tree or shrub or a tract of such vegetation.

SEAL   (1) A device having a raised design that can be stamped on clay or wax; OR, (2) A substance used to close or secure something or to prevent seepage of moisture or air; OR, (3) Any of various carnivorous sea mammals found in the Northern Hemisphere and having a sleek, torpedo-shaped body and limbs adapted for swimming; OR, (4) A guarantee or pledge.

sound-alikes ACCORD – To conform or agree; bring into harmony, to grant, especially as being due or appropriate. We also have... **A CHORD**, which in music is a combination of three or more usually concordant tones sounded simultaneously. OR, how about **A CORD**, a slender length of flexible material usually of twisted strands or fibers and used to bind, tie, connect, or support.

SEALER (1) A coat applied to prevent subsequent coats of paint or varnish from sinking in; OR, (2) One that is engaged in the hunting of seals.

SEDATE (1) Serenely deliberate, composed, and dignified in character or manner; OR, (2) To administer a sedative to, or to calm by means of such a drug.

SET (1) To put in a specified stable position; to place, adjust, restore, arrange, prescribe, establish, or fix at a given amount; OR, (2) *Sports:* - to position oneself in such a way as to be ready to start an advantageous movement; OR, (3) A group of things of the same kind or characteristic; OR, (4) The entire enclosure in which a movie is filmed; the sound stage; OR, (5) *Sports:* - a group of tennis games constituting one division of a match; OR, (6) Deliberate, intent, fixed by authority or custom.

SHADE (1) Light diminished in intensity as a result of the interception of the rays; partial darkness; OR, (2) Any of various devices used to reduce or screen light or heat; OR, (3) The degree to which a color is mixed with another color to create a different hue.

SHAM (1) Counterfeit, imitation; OR,
(2) An ornamental covering for a pillow.

SHED   (1) To lose a natural growth or covering by natural process; OR, (2) To pour fourth, fall off, or drop out; OR, (3) A small structure built for storage or shelter.

SHORE   (1) The land along the edge of an ocean, a sea, a lake, or a river; OR, (2) To provide support such as beams or timbers against a structure.

SHOT   (1) The firing or discharge of a weapon, such as a gun; OR, (2) *Sports:* - a kicked, thrown, or stroked attempt to score or assist toward scoring; OR, (3) *Informal:* - an attempt, a try, a guess, a chance at odds; OR, (4) Tiny lead or steel pellets, especially ones used in a shotgun cartridge; OR, (5) A single cinematic view or take; a developed photograph; OR, (6) A drink, especially a jigger of liquor; OR, (7) The past tense and past participle of SHOOT; OR, (8) *Informal:* - worn out; ruined.

SHOWER   (1) A brief fall of precipitation, such as rain, hail, or sleet; OR, (2) A fall of a group of objects, especially from the sky, as meteors; OR, (3) A party given by friends who bring gifts; OR, (4) A bath taken with sprayed water.

SIREN   (1) A device for making a loud harsh sound as a signal or warning; OR, (2) *Mythology:* - sea nymphs whose singing lured mariners to destruction; OR, (3) *Slang:* - a hot babe!

daffy-nition   Remember the three wise men; **ME**, **MYSELF**, and **I**.

SIZE (1) Any of a series of dimensions whereby manufactured articles, such as shoes and clothing, are classified; OR, (2) Any of several substances made from glue, wax, or clay and used as a filler for porous materials such as paper, cloth, or wall surfaces; OR, (3) Physical extent or bulk, dimensions.

SKATE (1) *Sports:* - metal frame and runner or rollers attached to shoe and used for gliding over ice or smooth surface; or to glide on same; OR, (2) *Marine:* - any of various rays having a flattened body and greatly expanded pectoral fins that extend around the head.

SKIPPER (1) *Nautical:* - the master of a ship; a coach, director, or other leader; OR, (2) One who skips - omits, leaves hastily, passes over, or fails to attend: *"Betty Lou was a notorious skipper of Friday classes."*

SLAM (1) To shut with force and loud noise; OR, (2) The winning of all, or all but one, of the tricks during the play of one hand of bridge and other card games.

SLEW (1) To turn, veer, or skid; OR, (2) The past tense of SLAY; OR, (3) *Informal:* - a large amount or number: *"A slew of complaints."*

SLIP (1) To move smoothly, quietly, stealthily, or gradually; OR, (2) To slide involuntarily and lose balance; OR, (3) To fall behind or into fault or error; OR, (4) A woman's undergarment worn under a dress; OR, (5) *Nautical:* - a docking place for a ship, between two piers; OR, (6) To put on or remove (clothing) easily or quickly; OR, (7) A part of a plant cut or broken off for grafting or planting; OR, (8) A small piece of paper, especially a small form, document, or receipt.

SLUG (1) A round bullet larger than buckshot; OR, (2) A small, sometimes illegal metal disk for use in vending or gambling machines in place of a coin; OR, (3) *Informal:* - a large gulp of liquid; OR, (4) Any of

small worm-like mollusks related to snails; OR,
(5) To strike heavily with the fist or a baseball bat.

SMACK   (1) To press together and open ones lips quickly and noisily, as in eating or tasting; OR, (2) Squarely and sharply; *"She fell smack on her head"*; OR, (3) Characteristic flavor; also: a slight trace; OR, (4) *Slang:* - Heroin.

SNAKE   (1) Any of numerous scaly, limbless, sometimes venomous reptiles having a long, tapering body and found in most tropical and temperate regions; OR, (2) A long, highly flexible metal wire or coil used for cleaning drains; OR, (3) A treacherous person.

SNARE   (1) To trap or use a trapping device, often consisting of a noose, used for capturing birds and small animals; OR, (2) *Music:* - the drum and any of the wires or cords stretched across the lower skin of a snare drum to increase reverberation.

SNARL   (1) To growl viciously while baring the teeth; OR, (2) A confused, complicated, or tangled situation or mess; a predicament.

SOCK   (1) A short stocking reaching a point between the ankle and the knee; OR, (2) *Informal:* - to put (money) away in a safe place for future use; OR, (3) To hit or strike forcefully; a hard blow or punch.

SOIL   (1) The top layer of the earth's surface, consisting of rock, mineral particles, and organic matter; OR, (2) To make dirty; tarnish, corrupt, or defile.

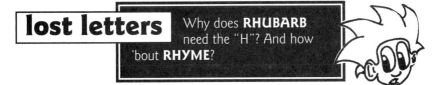

lost letters Why does **RHUBARB** need the "H"? And how 'bout **RHYME**?

39

SOLUTION (1) A homogeneous mixture of two or more substances, which may be solids, liquids, gases, or a
combination of these; OR, (2) The answer, method,
process or disposition of a problem.

SOUND (1) Transmitted vibrations of any frequency; OR,
(2) *Music:* - a distinctive style, as of an orchestra or a
singer; OR, (3) Free from defect, decay, or damage;
in good condition; OR, (4) *Logic:* - of or relating to
an argument in which all the premises are true and
the conclusion follows from the premises; OR,
(5) A long passage of water, larger that a strait or a
channel, connecting larger bodies of water.

SPADE (1) A sturdy shovel with a thick
handle and a heavy, flat blade;
OR, (2) A playing card with a
black, leaf-shaped figure; OR,
(3) *Offensive Slang:* - used
as a disparaging term for a
black person.

SPAR (1) *Nautical:* - a wooden or metal pole, such as a
mast, boom, yard-arm, or bowsprit, used to support
sails and rigging; OR, (2) To box for practice without
serious hitting.

SPELL (1) To name or write in order the letters constituting
a word; OR, (2) A word or formula believed to have
magic power; a trance; OR, (3) A compelling attrac-
tion, charm, or fascination; OR, (4) A short, indefi-
nite period of time, weather, work, or rest.

SPIKE (1) A long thick, sharp-pointed piece of wood or
metal; OR, (2) Metal projections from the sole and

heel of some athletic shoes; OR, (3) *Sports:* - in volleyball, action of driving the ball into the opponent's court at a sharp angle by jumping near the net; in football, the act of slamming the ball to the ground after scoring a touchdown; OR, (4) *Informal:* - to add alcoholic liquor to something non-alcoholic.

SPIT   (1) Saliva, or the act of expectorating saliva; OR, (2) A slender, pointed rod on which meat is impaled for broiling; OR, (3) Narrow point of land jutting out into a large body of water.

SPOKE   (1) One of the rods or braces connecting the hub and rim of a wheel; OR, (2) The past tense of SPEAK.

SPRAY   (1) Water or other liquid moving in a mass of dispersed droplets; OR, (2) A branch bearing buds, flowers, or berries.

SPRING   (1) The season of the year occurring between winter and summer in the Northern Hemisphere; a time of growth and renewal; OR, (2) The act or instance of jumping or leaping; OR, (3) A small stream of water flowing naturally from the earth; OR, (4) To move out of place; come loose or crack, as in parts of a mechanism or of wood; OR, (5) *Slang:* - to pay another's expenses: "he said he would spring for lunch"; OR, (6) An elastic device, such as a coil of wire, that regains its shape after being compressed or extended; elasticity, resilience.

SPRUCE   (1) Any of various coniferous evergreen trees having needle-like foliage, dropping cones, and a soft wood; OR, (2) To make neat, trim, and smart in appearance.

SQUASH   (1) Any of various tendril-bearing plants having fleshy edible fruit; OR, (2) To beat, squeeze, or press into a pulp; to crush; OR, (3) A racket game played in a closed court with a rubber ball.

STABLE   (1) Resistant to change of position or condition; steadfast; OR, (2) A building for the shelter and feeding of domestic animals; OR, (3) *Slang:* - All the racehorses or all of a group, such as athletes, under common management, authority, or ownership.

STAFF   (1) A stick or cane carried as an aid in walking or climbing; OR, (2) A group of assistants under another's authority;

STALK   (1) A stem or similar structure that supports a plant part, such as flower or leaf; OR, (2) To move threateningly, to track prey or quarry.

STALL   (1) A compartment for one domestic animal or one space for parking a vehicle within a shelter; OR, (2) A booth, cubicle, or stand used by a vendor; OR, (3) The sudden loss of power of an engine or of lift in an aircraft; OR, (4) To check the motion or progress of; bring to a standstill; OR, (5) A ruse or tactic used to mislead or delay.

STAPLE   (1) A basic commodity or product; OR, (2) A thin piece of wire that is driven by a device through sheets of paper, and the like, to serve as a fastening.

STEEP   (1) Having a sharp inclination; precipitous; OR, (2) To soak in liquid in order to cleanse, soften, or extract a given property.

STEER   (1) To guide with a rudder or wheel; OR, (2) To pursue a course of action; OR, (3) A young male bovine, castrated before sexual maturity and raised for beef.

sound-alikes CANOPIES – Draperies, awnings, or other rooflike coverings fastened over beds, thrones, or sacred things. Not to be confused with a **CAN O' PEAS**, a container full of round green veggies!

STEM	(1) The main stalk of a plant; OR, (2) A connection or supporting part as of a tobacco pipe, or a wine glass; OR, (3) *Music:* - the vertical line extending from the head of a note; OR, (4) To stop or check by or as if by damming.
STERN	(1) The rear part of a ship or boat; OR, (2) Hard or severe in manner or character, relentless.
STEW	(1) To cook (food) by simmering or boiling slowly; a dish created by this process consisting of meat or fish and vegetables with stock; OR, (2) *Informal:* - to be in a state of anxiety or agitation.
STICK	(1) A long slender piece of wood; OR, (2) To pierce with a pointed instrument; OR, (3) To fasten or attach with an adhesive, such as glue or tape; OR, (4) To be or become fixed or embedded in place.
STILL	(1) Low in sound, motionless, silent; OR, (2) An apparatus for distilling liquors, such as alcohol; OR, (3) Yet: *"He still loves her."*
STIR	(1) To mix, blend; OR, (2) To rouse, or excite; OR, (3) *Slang:* - prison.
STOLE	(1) *Ecclesiastical:* - a long scarf worn over the left shoulder by deacons and over both shoulders by priests and bishops while officiating; OR, (2) A woman's long scarf of cloth or fur worn about the shoulders; OR, (3) The past tense of STEAL.
STOOP	(1) To bend forward and down from the waist or the middle of the back; OR, (2) A small porch, platform, or staircase leading to an entrance.
STORE	(1) A place where merchandise is offered for sale; a shop; OR, (2) To place or leave in a safe location for preservation or future use: *"Squirrels store their acorns, and we squirrel away money!"*

STORY   (1) A usually fictional prose or verse narrative intended to interest or amuse the hearer or reader; a tale; OR, (2) A report, statement, or allegation of facts as in a news broadcast; OR, (3) A complete horizontal division of a building, constituting the area between two vertically adjacent levels.

STOUT   (1) Marked by boldness, bravery, or determination; firm and resolute; OR, (2) Strong in body, structure or substance; solid, sturdy, or substantial; OR, (3) A strong, very dark beer or ale.

STRAIN   (1) To pull, draw, stretch, exert, or tax beyond the proper or maximum limit; OR, (2) To draw off or remove by filtration; OR, (3) The collective descendants of common ancestors, a race, stock, line, or breed.

STRAND   (1) A piece of land bordering a body of water; a beach; OR, (2) To bring into or leave in a difficult or helpless position; OR, (3) A single filament, fiber, or thread or a complex of such material twisted together to form a cable, rope, thread, or yarn; OR, (4) A wisp or tress of hair.

STRAW   (1) Stalks of threshed grain, used as bedding and food for animals, for thatching (roofing), or for weaving or braiding, as into baskets; OR, (2) A slender tube for sucking up or sipping a liquid; OR, (3) A substitute for or preceding event, as a straw poll or candidate.

STRIP   (1) To remove, dismantle, or deprive of clothing, covering or parts; OR, (2) To deprive of honors, rank, office, privileges, or possessions; OR, (3) A long narrow piece, usually of uniform width, such as paper, beef, land, etc.; OR, (4) A frequently recurring illustrated cartoon generally set in a row of boxes.

STROKE   (1) The striking of a gong or bell, as to indicate time; OR, (2) The sudden occurrence of lightning, or luck; OR, (3) The sudden loss of brain function caused by a blockage or rupture of a blood vessel; OR, (4) Any of a series of movements, such as a piston or pen; the swinging of a bat, club, racket, oar, or arm; OR, (5) To rub lightly with the hand or something held in the hand; OR, (6) *Informal:* - to behave flatteringly toward in order to restore confidence.

STUD   (1) An ornamental button or earring mounted on a slender post; OR, (2) The upright post of a wall for supporting sheets of lath or wallboard; OR, (3) Any of various protruding pins or pegs; OR, (4) Small metal cleats in snow tires or crosspieces on tire chains; OR, (5) Male animal used for breeding; OR, (6) *Slang:* - a man regarded as virile and sexually active.

STUDY   (1) The pursuit of knowledge, as by reading, observation, or research; OR, (2) A room intended or equipped for studying or writing.

STUNT   (1) To hinder the normal growth or progress of; OR, (2) A feat displaying strength, skill, or daring, sometimes done for publicity.

pun-ishment What would you call a sobbing sovereign?

The PRINCE OF WAILS!!

STY	(1) An enclosure for swine; a filthy place; OR, (2) (or STYE) An inflammation of one or more sebaceous glands of an eyelid.
SUB	(1) A prefix meaning below; OR, (2) *Informal:* - Submarine; OR, (3) *Informal:* - Submarine sandwich; OR, (4) *Informal:* - Substitute.
SWALLOW	(1) To cause to pass through the mouth and throat into the stomach; OR, (2) *Slang:* - to believe without question: *"They swallowed the flimsy alibi."*; OR, (3) Any of various small, graceful, swift-flying birds having long, pointed wings, a usually notched or forked tail and noted for their regular migrations in large numbers, often over long distances.
TAB	(1) A projection, flap, or short strip attached to an object to facilitate opening, handling, or identification; OR, (2) *Informal:* - a bill or check, such as for a meal in a restaurant, or multiple drinks in a bar or tavern.
TACK	(1) A small, sharp nail with a broad flat head; OR, (2) *Nautical:* - the position of a vessel relative to the direction of the wind; OR, (3) A large, loose stitch made as a temporary binding; OR, (4) The devices for harnessing a horse, including the bridle and saddle.
TACKY	(1) Slightly adhesive or gummy to the touch; sticky; OR, (2) Distasteful, offensive; OR, (3) Neglected and in a state of disrepair.

how about this...

PIER PRESSURE – A yacht pressing against the dock!

TAG　　　　(1) A strip of leather, paper, metal, or plastic attached to something or someone to identify, classify, or label; OR, (2) The refrain or last lines of a song, poem, or a speech in a play; OR, (3) *Games:* - a children's game in which one player pursues the others until he or she is able to touch (or "tag") one of them, who in turn becomes "it," the pursuer; OR, (4) *Sports:* - in baseball, to touch a base or a player with the ball in order to put that player out; in football, to touch the ball carrier instead of tackling, as in touch football.

TAN　　　　(1) To become brown or tawny from exposure to the sun; OR, (2) To convert hide into leather, as by treating with tannin; OR, (3) *Informal:* - to spank or beat.

TAP　　　　(1) To strike gently with a light blow or blows; OR, (2) A metal plate attached to the toe and heel of a shoe, as for tap-dancing; OR, (3) To select, as for membership in an organization; designate; OR, (4) A valve or spigot used to regulate delivery of a fluid at the end of a pipe.

TAR　　　　(1) A dark, oily material, produced by the distillation of organic substances such as wood, coal, or peat; OR, (2) *Informal:* - a sailor.

TART　　　　(1) Having a sharp, pungent taste; OR, (2) Sharp or bitter in tone or meaning; cutting; OR (3) A small open pie with a sweet filling, as of custard or cooked fruit; OR, (4) A prostitute (generally British/English).

TATTOO　　(1) A permanent mark or design made on the skin with an indelible pigment; OR, (2) A signal sounded on a drum or bugle to summon soldiers or sailors to their quarters at night; OR, (3) *Scotland:* - a festival of military bands (esp. bagpipes) and units.

TEMPLE　　(1) A building dedicated to religious ceremonies or worship; OR, (2) The flat region on either side of the forehead.

47

TEND	(1) To be disposed or inclined toward; OR, (2) To have the care of, watch over, look after, or manage.
TENDER	(1) Easily crushed or bruised; fragile, sensitive, painful, easily hurt; OR, (2) An offer of money or service in payment of an obligation; OR, (3) A formal offer, as for goods or services, at a specified cost or rate; a bid; OR, (4) A vessel attendant on other vessels; a railroad car attached to the rear of a locomotive to carry fuel and water.
TERMINAL	(1) Of forming a limit, a boundary, an extremity, or an end; OR, (2) *Botany:* - growing at the end of a stem, branch, stalk, or similar part; OR, (3) Causing or approaching death; fatal: *"terminal cancer"*; OR, (4) *Electricity:* - a position in a circuit or device at which a connection is normally established or broken; OR, (5) Either end of a railroad or other transportation line; a terminus; OR, (6) *Computers:* - a device through which data or information can enter or leave a computer system.
TILL	(1) To prepare land for the raising of crops, as by plowing and harrowing; OR, (2) A drawer or compartment for money, as in a store.
TILLER	(1) One who cultivates land for planting; OR, (2) *Nautical:* - a lever used to turn a rudder and steer a boat.
TIP	(1) The end, or a thing to be fitted to the end, of a pointed or projecting object; OR, (2) To push or knock over, overturn or topple; OR, (3) *Sports:* - to tap or deflect the ball or puck; OR, (4) A small sum of extra money given to someone for performing a service; OR, (5) A piece of confidential, advance, or inside information.

TIRE

(1) To diminish the strength or energy of; fatigue; OR, (2) *Automotive:* - a rubber wheel cover reinforced with cords of nylon, fiberglass, or other material and filled with air.

TOAST

(1) To brown the surface of, by placing in a toaster or an oven or close to a fire; OR, (2) The act of raising a glass and drinking in honor of or to the health of a person or event.

TOLL

(1) A fixed charge or tax for a privilege, especially for passage across a bridge or along a road; OR, (2) To sound a bell slowly at regular intervals; OR, (3) A service charge for long distance phone calls; OR, (4) The amount or extent of loss or destruction, as in a disaster.

TOP

(1) The uppermost part, point, surface, or end; OR, (2) Something, such as a lid or cap, that covers; OR, (3) *Baseball:* - the first half of every inning; OR, (4) To exceed or surpass, be at the head; OR, (5) A toy having one end tapered to a point, allowing it to be spun.

TRAIN

(1) A series of connected railroad cars; OR, (2) A long line of people, animals, or vehicles; OR, (3) Part of a gown that trails behind the wearer; OR, (4) To coach in or accustom to a mode of behavior or performance.

TROLL

(1) To fish by trailing a baited line behind a moving boat; OR, (2) A supernatural creature of Scandinavian folklore.

lost letters
How come we don't hear the "K" in words like **KNOB** and **KNOLL**??

UTTER
(1) To send forth as a sound; OR, (2) To articulate words; pronounce or speak; OR, (3) Complete, absolute; entire.

VAMP
(1) *Music:* - to improvise as to fill time within a performance; OR, (2) A woman who uses her charm or wiles to seduce and exploit men.

VAULT
(1) An arch of stone, brick, or concrete, supporting a ceiling or roof; OR, (2) A room or compartment, often built of steel, for safekeeping valuables; OR, (3) To jump or leap over, especially with the aid of a support, such as the hands or a pole.

VET
(1) *Informal:* - a veterinarian; OR, (2) *Informal:* - a veteran.

VOLUME
(1) A book or one of a set of books; OR, (2) The issues of a periodical, usually covering one calendar year; OR, (3) The amount of space occupied by a three-dimensional object or fluid; OR, (4) Amount, quantity: a low volume of sales; a large volume of lumber; OR, (5) The degree of loudness of a sound.

WAFFLE
(1) A light, crisp batter cake baked in a waffle iron; OR, (2) *Informal:* - to speak or write evasively.

WAGE
(1) Payment for labor or services usually according to contract; OR, (2) To engage in a war or campaign, for example.

WAKE
(1) To become or remain awake; OR, (2) A watch or guard, as over a corpse; OR, (3) The visible track of turbulence left by something moving through water.

WELL   (1) A deep hole or shaft sunk into the earth to obtain water, oil, or gas; OR, (2) An enclosed space for receiving and holding something, such as the retracted wheels of an airplane; OR, (3) Not ailing, infirm, or diseased; healthy; OR, (4) Thoroughly, completely, perfectly, clearly.

WILL   (1) The mental powers manifested as wishing, choosing, desiring, or intending; OR, (2) A legal declaration of how a person wishes his or her possessions to be disposed of after death; OR, (3) Auxiliary verb to express desire, willingness, action, capability, probability, ad nauseum: *"I will stop listing these now!"*

YAK   (1) A wild, shaggy-haired ox of the mountains of central Asia, used as a work animal or raised for meat and milk; OR, (2) *Slang:* - to talk persistently and meaninglessly; chatter.

YARD   (1) A fundamental unit of length equal to 3 feet, or 36 inches; OR, (2) A long spar attached loosely to a mast to support the head of a square sail; OR, (3) A tract of ground, often enclosed, usually covered with grass and flowers; OR, (4) A storage area, generally for large equipment or machinery.

YARN   (1) A continuous strand of twisted threads of natural or synthetic material, such as wool or nylon, used in weaving or knitting; OR, (2) *Informal:* - a long, often elaborate narrative of real or fictitious adventures; an entertaining tale.

YEN   (1) A strong desire or inclination; a yearning or craving; OR, (2) A basic unit of currency in Japan.

sound-alikes   **TEN "10"** – Commandments; little Indians; cents a dance; percenter (an agent); gymnastics perfect score; knockout count in boxing; perfect woman walking along the beach; and the base for the decimal system. Can you think of more?

HOMONYMS "A"

HOMONYMS "B"

This grouping contains words which have the same pronunciation, but different spellings and definitions.

ADDS	Is or serves as an addition; augments; performs the arithmetical operation of addition; *"I guess it all adds up."*
ADZ	An ax-like tool with a curved blade at right angles to the handle, used for dressing wood.

———————————————— ℮ ————————————————

ADE	(Suffix) A sweetened beverage such as with lemon or orange.
AID	To help; support; an assistant or assistance; a device that assists; to give help.
AIDE	An aide-de-camp; a helper. *"She aided by giving ade to the aide."*

———————————————— ℮ ————————————————

AIL	To feel ill or have pain; to make ill or cause pain.
ALE	A fermented, bitter alcoholic beverage similar to beer.

———————————————— ℮ ————————————————

AIR	A colorless, odorless, tasteless, gaseous mixture, mainly nitrogen (78%) and oxygen (21%); the earth's atmosphere; *Music:* - a melody or tune.
HEIR	A person who inherits or will inherit the estate, rank, title, or office of another.

———————————————— ℮ ————————————————

AIRY	Of or like air; lofty; open; speculative; light-hearted; gay.
AERIE	A nest, as of an eagle, built on a high place.

———————————————— ℮ ————————————————

AISLE	A passageway between rows of seats, as in an auditorium or airplane.
ISLE	An island, especially a small one.

ALL   Being or representing the entire or total number, amount or quantity. *"All the windows are open."*

AWL   A pointed tool for making holes, as in wood or leather.

ALLOWED   Admitted, conceded; permitted; *"I allowed her to go."*

ALOUD   Using the voice as to read text, or as in conversation.

ALTAR   An elevated place or structure before or upon which religious ceremonies may be performed.

ALTER   To change; modify; to adjust, as a garment; to neuter an animal.

ANSWER   A reply, solution, response, or retaliation.

ANSER   *Latin:* - of or belonging to the subfamily comprising geese.

ANT   Any of various social insects of the family Formicidae, characteristically having wings only in the males and fertile females and living in colonies with a complex social organization. *Slang:* - a state of restless impatience; *"She has ants in her pants."*

Mom

Mom's sister

AUNT   The sister of one's father or mother; the wife of one's uncle.

ANTE   The stake each poker player puts into the pool before receiving a hand or new cards; *Earlier:* - before.

ANTI	Opposite; opposed to; counteracting; inverse.

ARC	Something shaped like a curve or an arch; a segment of a circle; a luminous electric discharge.
ARK	*Bible:* - the boat built by Noah; the chest containing the Ten Commandments.

BAIL	Security, usually money, supplied as a guarantee that an arrested person will appear for trial; to remove water from a boat using a container.
BALE	A large, tightly bound package of raw or finished material.

BAIT	Food or other lure used to catch fish or trap animals; to entice; torment or tease.
BATE	To lessen the force of; to moderate.

BALD	Lacking hair on the head; lacking a natural or usual covering; bare; plain or blunt.
BAWLED	Sobbed or cried out loudly; bellowed.

BALL	A formal gathering for social dancing; *Slang:* - an extremely enjoyable time or experience: *"We had a ball during our vacation."* A spherical or almost spherical body; *Sports/Games:* - any of various rounded, moveable objects used in various athletic activities that can be moved, thrown, rolled, hit, or kicked in a particular manner: a low ball; a fair ball.
BAWL	To cry or sob loudly; wail; to scold harshly.

BARE	Naked; exposed to view; lacking the usual furnishings, equipment, or decoration.
BEAR	To carry, to be equipped with; any of the various large omnivorous mammals having a shaggy coat and a short tail; a grouchy person.

BASE	A foundation; a center of organization, supply, or activity; headquarters; morally bad; lowly; inferior. *Baseball*: - any one of the four corners of the infield marked by a bag or plate.
BASS	A deep sound or tone.

BE	To exist; to take place; to equal in identity; to belong.
BEE	Any of several winged, hairy-bodied, stinging insects that gather nectar and pollen from which some species produce honey; a social gathering where people work together or compete.

BEACH	The shore of a body of water, especially sandy or pebbly.
BEECH	A deciduous tree having smooth gray bark, simple leaves, and triangular nuts enclosed in prickly burrs.

BEAT	To strike repeatedly; to punish by hitting; to shape by blows; to mix rapidly; fatigued; a rhythmic stress, as in music or verse.
BEET	A cultivated plant with a fleshy dark-red edible root.

BEAU	A suitor; a dandy.
BOW	A curve or arch; a weapon to shoot or project arrows; a decorative knot; *Music*: - a rod strung with horsehair, used in playing the violin and other string instruments.

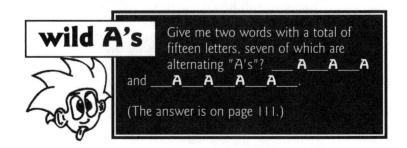

wild A's Give me two words with a total of fifteen letters, seven of which are alternating "A's"? ___ **A** ___ **A** ___ **A** and ___ **A** ___ **A** ___ **A** ___ **A** ___.

(The answer is on page 111.)

BEEN	Past participle of BE.
BIN	A container or closed space for storage.

❧

BELL	A hollow metallic device that makes a ringing sound when struck.
BELLE	An attractive and admired girl or woman.

❧

BIGHT	A loop in a rope; a bend or curve in a shoreline.
BITE	To cut, grip, or tear with, or as if with, the teeth; to pierce with fangs.
BYTE	*Computer Science:* - a sequence of adjacent bits operated on as a unit; the amount of memory needed to store one character, 8 or 16 bits.

❧

BLEW	The past tense of BLOW; *"He blew up the balloon."*
BLUE	Any of a group of colors whose hue is that of a clear daytime sky; downhearted; gloomy.

❧

BLOC	A group of nations, parties, or persons united by common interests.
BLOCK	A solid piece of a hard substance, such as wood or stone, having one or more flat sides; a stand used at an auction; a set of like items; a section of a city or town; to obstruct.

❧

BOAR	An uncastrated male pig; a wild pig.
BOER	A Dutch colonist or descendant of a Dutch colonist in South Africa.
BORE	To make a hole in or through with, or as if with, a drill. A passage made by drilling; to make weary by being dull, repetitive, or tedious.

BOARD	A flat length of sawed lumber; a flat surface on which a game is played; food and lodging provided for a charge; to enter a ship, train, or plane.
BORED	The past tense of BORE; *"He bored holes in the board."*

BOARDER	One who boards, especially one who pays a stipulated sum in return for regular meals or for meals and lodging; *Sports:* - one who rides a skateboard or a snowboard.
BORDER	A part that forms the outer edge of something such as fabric or a garden or a walkway; the line or frontier area separating political divisions or geographic regions; a boundary.

BOLE	A tree trunk.
BOLL	A seed pod, especially of cotton and flax.
BOWL	A rounded hollow vessel for food or fluids; the curved hollow part of a pipe; a large solid ball rolled in certain games; to roll a ball in bowling.

BOY	A male child or youth; used to express mild elation or disgust.
BUOY	A float, often having a bell or light, moored in water as a warning of danger or as a marker for a channel; to hearten or inspire.

BRAKE	A device for slowing or stopping motion by contact friction; a thicket.
BREAK	To separate into or reduce to pieces by sudden force; to make or become unusable or inoperative; to give way, collapse; to surpass or out-do; to reduce in rank.

* SCREECH *

BREAD	A staple food made chiefly from moistened, leavened flour or meal kneaded and baked; food in general; *Slang:* - money.
BRED	The past tense of BREED; *"A horse well bred is worth more bread."*

⟡

BRIDAL	Of or relating to a bride or a marriage ceremony; nuptial.
BRIDLE	A harness, consisting of a headstall, bit, and reins, fitted about a horse's head and used to restrain or guide the animal.

⟡

BROACH	To bring up a subject for discussion or debate; to announce plans; a spit for roasting meat.
BROOCH	A relatively large decorative pin or clasp.

⟡

BURRO	A small donkey used as a pack animal.
BURROW	A hole or tunnel dug in the ground by an animal for habitation or refuge.

⟡

BUS	A long motor vehicle for carrying passengers.
BUSS	A kiss.

⟡

BUT	Contrary to expectation; on the contrary; yet.
BUTT	To hit with the head or horns; to join or be joined end to end; an object of ridicule; a large cask; the unburned end of a cigarette or cigar.

sound-alikes DEPOSE – To remove from office or power. But what about...
DEPOTS, meaning railroad or bus stations, or the storage installations for military equipment and/or supplies?

59

BUY   To acquire in exchange for money; to acquire by sacrifice.

BY   Next to; with the use of; not later than; according to.

BYE   A side issue; used to express farewell.

CANTER   A smooth gait of a horse, slower than a gallop, but faster than a trot.

CANTOR   The Jewish religious official who leads the musical part of a service.

CAPITAL   The town, city, or district that is the official seat of government; wealth; first rate; serious; an upper-case letter.

CAPITOL   The building in which a legislature meets: *"The capitol building in the capital."*

CARAT   A unit of weight for precious stones, equal to 200 mg.

KARAT   A unit for expressing proportion of gold in an alloy equal to 1/24 part of pure gold.

CARROT   A plant widely cultivated for its edible taproot; a fleshy orange root, eaten as a vegetable; a reward or inducement.

CART   A small wheeled vehicle typically pushed or pulled by hand or by animals used for transporting goods.

KART   *Sports:-* a miniature car used in racing.

CASH   Money in the form of bills or coins paid at the time of purchase or delivery; to pay or obtain cash for.

CACHE   A hiding place for concealment and safekeeping, as of valuables; a store of goods or material concealed in a hiding place.

CAST   To throw or fling; to shed or discard; to deposit or indicate; to form by molding; to compute; actors in a

	theatrical presentation; surgical dressing used to immobilize a fractured body part.
CASTE	A social class separated from others by distinctions of heredity, rank, wealth, or profession; status.

CEILING	The upper interior surface of a room; an upper limit, especially set by regulation, *"wage and price ceilings."* The highest altitude under particular weather conditions from which the ground is still visible.
SEALING	The act of affixing a seal to in order to prove authenticity, accuracy, legal weight, quality, or other standard. To close, make fast, fill up, and/or apply a waterproof coating to.

CELLAR	An underground room beneath a building; a stock of wines.
SELLER	One who exchanges wares for money or its equivalent; one who promotes or convinces.

CENTS	The plural of CENT; U.S. currency - 1/100 of one dollar.
SENSE	Any of the faculties of hearing, sight, smell, touch, taste and equilibrium; correct judgement.

CEREAL	A grass such as wheat, oats, or corn, whose starchy grains are used as food; a food prepared from such grains.
SERIAL	Arranged in a series; published or produced in installments.

lost letters Has anybody ever heard the "B" in **CRUMB**, **DEBT**, **DOUBT**, **SUBTLE**, **JAMB**, **LAMB**, **NUMB**, **PLUMB**, or **THUMB**? If we had a few more silent bees we wouldn't have much honey.

CHASED	The past tense of CHASE: *"One being chased cannot chase his or her chaser."*
CHASTE	Morally pure; modest; abstaining from illicit sexual acts or thoughts.

———————————— ❧ ————————————

CHEAP	Of little value; inexpensive; achieved with little effort; vulgar; stingy.
CHEEP	A faint shrill sound like that made by a young bird.

———————————— ❧ ————————————

CHOIR	An organized company of singers, as in a church; a group of similar orchestral instruments.
QUIRE	A set of 24 or sometimes 25 sheets of paper of the same size and stock; 1/20 of a ream.

———————————— ❧ ————————————

CHOOSE	To decide on and pick out; to select; to prefer above others.
CHEWS	The act of chewing, i.e. grinding and crushing with the teeth.

———————————— ❧ ————————————

CHORD	*Music:* -a combination of three or more usually harmonious tones sounded simultaneously.
CORD	A string of twisted strands or fibers; an insulated, flexible electric wire fitted with a plug; a reference to the spine; a unit quantity of cut wood.

———————————— ❧ ————————————

CHUTE	An inclined surface, trough, or passage down or through which some things may pass. *Slang:* - parachute.
SHOOT	To hit, wound, or kill with a missile; to discharge a weapon; to record on film; to begin to grow.

———————————— ❧ ————————————

CLAUSE	A distinct article, stipulation, or provision in a document, such as a contract.
CLAWS	The sharp, curved, nails on the toes of mammals, reptiles, or birds.

COARSE	Of inferior quality; lacking refinement; rough to the touch.
COURSE	The route or path taken by something; duration; a mode of action; a body of prescribed studies; a part of a meal.

COAX	To persuade or try to persuade by pleading or flattery; cajole.
COKES	Multiple units of a popular soft drink.

COOP	A cage; to confine.
COUPE	An enclosed two-door automobile.

CORAL	The sharp, stony or horny material that forms the skeleton of colonies of sea polyps; a deep pink color.
CHORAL	Of or for a chorus or choir.

CORE	The hard or fibrous central part of certain fruits containing seeds; the most important part; the part of a nuclear reactor where fission occurs.
CORPS	A specialized branch or department of the armed forces; a body of persons under common direction.

CORRAL	An enclosure for confining livestock.
CHORALE	A harmonized hymn; a chorus or choir.

COUNCIL	An assembly of persons called together for deliberation or discussion.
COUNSEL	The act of exchanging opinions and ideas; consultation; advice or guidance; a plan of action.

CREAK	To make a prolonged squeaking sound.
CREEK	A small stream, often a tributary to a river.

CUE	A long tapered rod used to strike the cue ball in billiards and pool; a word or signal, as in a play, to prompt another actor's speech or entrance; a reminder or hint.
QUEUE	A line of waiting people or vehicles; a long braid of hair worn hanging down the back of the neck.

CURRANT	Any of a genus of shrubs having edible, variously colored berries; a small raisin.
CURRENT	Belonging to the present time; the part of a body of liquid or gas that is in flow; the flow of electrons.

DAM	A barrier built across a waterway to control the flow of water; a female parent of a four-legged animal.
DAMN	To criticize adversely; condemn; to bring to ruin; to swear at.

DEAR	Loved and cherished; *"my dearest friend."* Highly esteemed or regarded. Used in direct address especially in salutation; *"Dear Maria, ..."*
DEER	Any of various hoofed ruminant mammals of the family Cervidae, having deciduous antlers borne chiefly by the males. The deer family also includes the elk, moose, caribou, and reindeer.

how about this...

SOUP OR SALAD ?
This is what the waitress in a restaurant might ask you. Or did it sound like **SUPER-SALAD**? Next time, give a listen.

DESERT	To leave empty or alone; abandon; to withdraw from responsibility or duty.
DESSERT	A usually sweet course or dish, as of fruit, ice cream, or pastry, served at the end of a meal.

―――――――――――――――――ℰ―――――――――――――――――

DIE	To cease living; expire; to cease existing by degrees; a device used for cutting out, forming, machining, punching, or stamping materials; a gaming cube marked on each side with from one to six dots.
DYE	A substance used to color or stain; a color imparted by dyeing.

―――――――――――――――――ℰ―――――――――――――――――

DO	To perform or execute; to fulfill; to produce; to bring about; to render; to work at; to get along.
DEW	Water droplets condensed from the air onto cool surfaces.
DUE	Payable immediately or on demand; owed as a debt or right; expected or scheduled; capable of being attributed.

―――――――――――――――――ℰ―――――――――――――――――

DOC	*Informal:* - doctor; abbr. for document.
DOCK	A pier or wharf; to clip the tail of an animal; a place for a defendant to stand or sit in a court of law.

―――――――――――――――――ℰ―――――――――――――――――

DOE	The female of a deer or certain other animals, such as the hare or kangaroo.
DOUGH	A soft thick mixture of flour and other ingredients that is kneaded, shaped, and baked, as bread, or pastry.
DO	The first note on the music scale: "*do-re-mi...*"

―――――――――――――――――ℰ―――――――――――――――――

DONE	The past participle of DO; completely accomplished or finished.
DUN	To make persistent demands for payment; a neutral brownish gray.

DUAL	Composed of two parts; double; having a double character or purpose.
DUEL	A prearranged formal combat between two persons, usually fought to settle a point of honor.

———————————————ꙮ———————————————

EARN	To gain for the performance of service or labor; to acquire or deserve as a result of effort or action; to yield as return or profit.
URN	A vessel that typically has the form of a vase on a pedestal and often is used to hold the ashes of the dead; a closed metal vessel having a spout for serving tea or coffee.

———————————————ꙮ———————————————

EAVE	The projecting overhang at the lower edge of a roof.
EVE	The evening or day preceding a special day, such as a holiday; the period immediately preceding a certain event: *"The eve of war."*

———————————————ꙮ———————————————

EERIE	Inspiring inexplicable fear or uneasiness; suggestive of the supernatural.
ERIE	A Native American people formerly inhabiting the south shore of Lake Erie.

———————————————ꙮ———————————————

EIGHT	The cardinal number equal to 7 + 1; the 8th in a set or sequence.
ATE	The past tense of EAT: *"He ate the whole pie."*

7 + 1 = 8

EL	An abbreviation for elevation; slang for "elevated train"; the twelfth letter of our alphabet.
ELL	A wing of a building at right angles to the main structure; the right-angled bend in a pipe or conduit.

⁂

EYE	An organ of vision or of light sensitivity; the ability to perceive or discern; a point of view; attention.
AYE	An affirmative vote or voter.

⁂

FACTS	The plural of FACT, things that have actually happened; acts, deeds, reality, truth, actuality; the state of things as they are.
FAX	To transmit printed matter or an image by electronic means; alteration of facsimile.

⁂

FAINT	Lacking strength or vigor; lacking brightness; indistinct; suddenly dizzy and weak causing a brief loss of consciousness.
FEINT	A feigned attack designed to draw defensive action away from an intended target; a deceptive action calculated to divert attention from one's real purpose.

⁂

FAIR	Beautiful; lovely; light in color; clear and sunny; unblemished; just; consistent with rules; moderately good; direct; straight; a gathering or exhibition, held at a specified time and place for the buying and selling of goods, usually accompanied by various competitions and entertainments, could also be a fundraiser.
FARE	A transportation charge, as for a bus or a taxi; as to food and drink: simple home-cooked fare; to get along: *"How are you faring with your project?"*

FAIRY
: A tiny imaginary being depicted as possessing magical powers; *Slang:* - derogatory reference to a homosexual.

FERRY
: To transport by boat across a body of water; the name applied to such boat.

FAKER
: One who is not genuine or authentic; a counterfeit; imposter or sham.

FAKIR
: A Muslim or Hindu mendicant who performs feats of magic or endurance.

FEAT
: A notable act or deed, especially of courage.

FEET
: The plural of FOOT: *"Feat, feet and fete do not equal a yard."*

FETE
: A festival or feast; an elaborate outdoor party.

FEW
: Not many; a limited number.

PHEW
: An exclamation expressing relief, disgust, surprise, etc.

FIR
: Any of a genus of erect evergreen trees having flattened needles and cones.

FUR
: The thick coat of soft hair covering the skin of various animals.

FLAIR
: A talent or aptitude; instinctive discernment or elegance.

FLARE
: To burst into intense, sudden flame; to expand or open outward; a device that produces a bright light for signaling or illumination.

how about this...

Do we really need the "W" in **SWORD**??

FLEA	Any of various small, wingless, bloodsucking insects that are parasitic on warm-blooded animals.
FLEE	To run away, as from trouble or danger; to vanish.

—————————— ℭ ——————————

FLEW	The past tense of FLY: *"The fly flew away."*
FLU	*Informal:-* Influenza; sickness.
FLUE	A pipe, tube, or channel for conveying hot air, gas, steam, or smoke, as in a chimney.

—————————— ℭ ——————————

FLOC	A mass formed in a fluid through precipitation or aggregation of suspended particles.
FLOCK	A group of animals that live, travel or feed together; a group of people under one leadership, such as members of a church; a fine texturing material; to coat with flock, as in wallpaper or Christmas trees.

—————————— ℭ ——————————

FLOUR	A fine powdery foodstuff obtained by grinding grain, e.g. wheat.
FLOWER	A plant cultivated for its blossoms; the period of highest development.

—————————— ℭ ——————————

FLOW	To move or run freely in, or as if in, a stream; to proceed steadily and easily.
FLOE	A large flat mass of floating ice.

—————————— ℭ ——————————

FOR	Used to indicate the object or purpose of an action or activity; on behalf of; used to indicate amount, extent, or duration.
FORE	At, in, near, or toward the front; used by a golfer to warn those ahead that a ball is headed in their direction.
FOUR	The cardinal number equal to 3 + 1; the 4th in a set or sequence.

FOREWORD A preface or introductory note, especially in a book.
FORWARD At, near, belonging to, or located in the front; going, tending, or moving toward the front; bold; mentally, physically, or socially advanced.

FORTH Forward or onward.
FOURTH One that is number four in a countable series; one of four equal parts.

FOUL Offensive to the senses; revolting, rotten or putrid; morally detestable; *Sports:* - an infraction of the rules.
FOWL A bird used as food or hunted as game.

FREES Releases a being or object from con-straints.
FREEZE To reach the temper-ature at which a given liquid turns to a solid; to become unable to act or react, as from fear or shyness.

Brrrr!"

FRIAR A man who is a member of a mendicant Roman Catholic order; brother.
FRYER One that fries; as a deep utensil equipped with a bas-ket and used for frying foods; a young chicken suit-able for frying.

GAEL A Celtic inhabitant of Scotland, Ireland, or the Isle of Man.
GALE A very strong wind; a forceful outburst, as of laughter.

GAIT	A way of moving on foot; a rate of pace; any of the ways a horse can move by lifting the feet in different order or rhythm.
GATE	A structure that can be swung, drawn, or lowered to block an entry or passageway.

—————————— ℯ ——————————

GALL	Bitterness of feeling; rancor; something bitter to endure; outrageous insolence.
GAUL	A Celt of Ancient Gaul; a French person.

—————————— ℯ ——————————

GOPHER	Any of various short-tailed, burrowing rodents of the family Geomyidae of North America, having fur lined external cheek pockets; any of various ground squirrels of the genus Citellus of North American prairies.
GOFER	*Slang:* - an employee who runs errands in addition to performing regular duties (alteration of 'go for').

—————————— ℯ ——————————

GRATE	To shred; to make or cause to make a harsh rasping sound; to irritate; a framework of parallel or latticed bars over an opening; assembled metal bars to hold fuel or food in a stove or fireplace.
GREAT	Very large in size, quantity, or number; remarkable in extent; of outstanding importance; very good; first rate.

—————————— ℯ ——————————

GUEST	One who is the recipient of hospitality at the home or table of another.
GUESSED	Having predicted or assumed (a result or an event) without sufficient information.

—————————— ℯ ——————————

GUILD	An association of persons of the same trade formed to protect common interests and maintain standards.
GILD	To cover with or as if with a thin layer of gold to give an often deceptively attractive appearance.

GUISE	An outward appearance or aspect, semblance; a false appearance or pretense.
GUYS	Ropes, chains, or rods attached to something, as braces or guides; *Informal:* - persons of either sex.

HAIL	Precipitation in the form of pellets of ice and hard snow; to salute or greet; to signal or call out to.
HALE	Sound in health; free from defect.

HAIR	A fine thread-like out-growth from the skin of a mammal; a minute distance or narrow margin.
HARE	A mammal similar to a rabbit but having longer ears and legs.

HALL	A corridor or passageway in a building; a large entrance room or vestibule; a lobby; the building or large room for public gatherings or entertainment.
HAUL	To pull or drag forcibly; tug. *Informal:* - to compel to go: "*He was hauled into court.*"

HANGAR	A shelter, especially for housing or repairing aircraft.
HANGER	One who hangs something, a paper hanger; a contrivance to which something hangs or by which something is hung, such as a garment.

HART	*British:* Stag (male deer).
HEART	The chambered, muscular organ that pumps blood received from the veins into the arteries, maintaining the flow of blood through the circulatory system.

HAY	Grass or other plants cut and dried for fodder; to mow and cure grass and herbage for hay.
HEY	Used to attract attention or to express surprise, appreciation, wonder, or pleasure.

HEAL	To restore to or regain health or soundness; to cure.
HEEL	The rounded posterior portion of the sole of human's (and other vertebrates) foot; the crusty end of a loaf of bread; a two-faced person; a command, as to a dog, to walk behind.

HEAR	To perceive by the ear; to learn by hearing; to attend.
HERE	As or in this place; response to a roll call, attract attention, command to an animal.

HEARD	The past tense and past participle of HEAR; ever heard a herd of cattle?
HERD	A group of animals, as domestic cattle, kept or living together; a crowd.

HEROIN	A white, odorless, bitter, crystalline compound derived from morphine that is a highly addictive narcotic.
HEROINE	A woman noted for courage and daring action or noted for special achievement, a female hero.

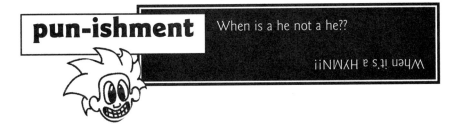

pun-ishment   When is a he not a he??

When it's a HYMN!!

HI	Informal greeting meaning "hello."
HIE	To go quickly; hasten.
HIGH	Relatively great in elevation; at or near a peak; piercing in tone or pitch; eminent in rank; intoxicated; a transmission's highest range of output speeds.

HIGHER	As in, or to a loftier position, level, or degree.
HIRE	To engage the services or use of for a fee.

HIM	A pronoun; the objective case of HE: *"They chose him."*
HYMN	A song of praise or thanksgiving.

HOARD	A supply hidden or stored for future use; to accumulate.
HORDE	A throng or swarm; crowd.

HOARSE	Rough and harsh in sound.
HORSE	A large hoofed animal having a long mane and tail, domesticated for riding and for drawing or carrying loads; a piece of gymnastic equipment used for vaulting.

HOLE	An opening into or through something; a hollow place, as a pit or cave; an animal's burrow; an ugly or depressing place; a bad situation; a goal in each of the 18 sections of a golf match.
WHOLE	Containing all parts; complete; not divided; constituting the full amount, extent, or duration; at full health.

HOLEY	Having a hole or holes.
HOLY	Of or associated with a divine power; sacred; worthy of veneration or awe; spiritually pure.

HOUR	A division of time, one of the twenty-four parts of a day; sixty minutes.
OUR	The possessive form of WE; belonging to, or done by us: *"Our hour is yet to come."*

IDLE	Not employed or busy; not in use or operation; lacking substance or basis.
IDOL	An image used as an object of worship; one that is adored.

JAM	To squeeze or lock into a tight, or unworkable position; to block or clog; a preserve made from fruit boiled with sugar; *Music:* - to play improvisationally.
JAMB	One of the vertical posts on a door or window frame.

KERNEL	A grain or seed, as of cereal grass; the inner, usually edible seed of a nut or fruit stone; the central part.
COLONEL	A military rank above Lieutenant Colonel and below Brigadier General.

KNEAD	To mix and work into a uniform mass especially with the hands; to massage.
NEED	A lack of something required or desirable; necessity; poverty.
KNEED	Used the knee to inflict damage or as a defense.

KNEE	The joint between the thigh and the lower leg.
NEE	Born; birth name.

KNEW	The past tense of KNOW. (I knew you'd know that.)
NEW	Not old; never used or worn before; unfamiliar, different from before; rejuvenated.
GNU	A large bearded African antelope with curved horns.

KNOT	A fastening made by tying together lengths of material, such as a rope, in a prescribed way; *Nautical:* - a marine unit of speed approximately equal to 1.15 statute miles per hour.
NOT	In no way; to no degree; used to express negation, denial, refusal, or prohibition.

KNOW	To perceive directly with the mind or senses; to regard as true; to be capable of or skilled in; to have learned, experienced, recognized, or be acquainted with.
NO	Used to express refusal, denial, disbelief, or disagreement; quantity of zero: *"Yes, we have no bananas!"*

KNOWS	See KNOW ; - *"He knows right from wrong."*
NOES	Negative responses or votes.
NOSE	The part of the face that contains the nostrils and organs of smell and forms the beginning of the respiratory tract; the forward end of an aircraft.

LADE	To load with cargo; to burden, weigh down.
LAID	The past tense and past participle of LAY.

LAM	To escape, as from prison; flight, especially from the law; to give a thorough beating to; thrash; strike; wallop.
LAMB	A young sheep; a sweet mild-mannered person.

LAMA — A buddhist monk of Tibet or Mongolia.

LLAMA — A South American mammal related to the camel, raised for its soft fleece wool and used as a beast of burden (pronounced "YAMA" in correct Spanish).

LANE — A narrow way or road; a set passage or course, as for vehicles, or ships.

LAIN — The past participle of LIE.

LAY — To cause to lie down; to put or set down; to produce and deposit (eggs); to devise; the past tense of LIE (and that's no fib).

LEI — A garland of flowers usually worn around the neck in Hawaii.

LEAD — (lĕd) A malleable bluish-white, dense metallic element used in solder, radiation shields, and alloys; a weight used to make soundings; cased in bullets and pencils.

LED — The past tense and past participle of LEAD (lĕd); guided, conducted, escorted, or directed.

LEAK — The escape of something through a breach or flaw; e.g. leak of fluid or information.

LEEK — An edible plant with a white slender bulb and dark-green leaves, related to the onion.

LEAN	To bend or cause to bend away from the vertical; to incline one's weight so as to be supported; to have a tendency or preference; flesh containing little or no fat; not productive.
LIEN	The right to take and hold or sell the property of a debtor as security or payment for a debt.

LEVEE	An embankment raised to prevent a river from over-flowing.
LEVY	To impose or collect by legal authority (as taxes); to draft into military service; to declare and wage war.

LIAR	One who tells lies.
LYRE	A stringed instrument of the harp family, especially in ancient Greece.

LIE	To place oneself in a flat, horizontal or recumbent position; a false statement deliberately presented as being true; a falsehood.
LYE	A caustic liquid obtained by leaching wood ashes; concentrated potassium or sodium hydroxide.

LOAD	A supported weight or mass; something carried; the force to which a structure is subjected; heavy responsibility; burden.
LODE	A vein of ore or mineral deposited between layers of rock.

how about this... How come the **ch** sound in **CHALK** has a different sound than the **ch** in **CHEMIST**??

LOCKS	Devices operated by a key, combination, or keycard and used, as on a door, for holding, closing, or securing; sections of a canal closed off with gates for raising or lowering the water level; lengths or curls of hair.
LOX	Smoked salmon.

LOOT	Valuables pillaged in time of war; spoils; stolen goods; to pillage.
LUTE	A stringed instrument having a body shaped like a pear sliced lengthwise and a neck with a fretted fingerboard that is usually bent just below the tuning pegs.

MACH	The ratio of the speed of an object to the speed of sound in the surrounding medium, e.g. an aircraft moving twice as fast as the speed of sound is said to be traveling at Mach 2.
MOCK	To treat with ridicule, scorn, or contempt; deride; simulated; sham; *"A mock battle."*

MADE	The past tense and past participle of MAKE (having produced something).
MAID	An unmarried girl or woman; a female servant.

MAIL	Materials, such as letters and packages, handled in a postal system; flexible armor composed of chain or scales.
MALE	Of or being the sex that produces germ cells which fertilize the eggs of females, a male individual.

MAIN	Most important; chief; the principal pipe or conduit in a system for conveying water, gas, oil, or other utility.
MANE	The long hair growing from the neck of certain animals, such as the horse and male lion; a long thick growth of human hair.

MAIZE	A variety of corn.
MAZE	An intricate, confusing network of interconnecting pathways, as in a garden; something made up of many confused or conflicting elements.

MALL	A large, often enclosed shopping complex containing various businesses.
MAUL	A heavy long-handled hammer used to drive stakes or wedges; to injure as if by beating: *"The boxer mauled the other fighter."*

MANTEL	An ornamental facing or protruding shelf over a fire-place.
MANTLE	A loose sleeveless outer garment (cloak); a device in gas lamps that glows brightly when heated by the flame.

MARSHALL	A military officer of the highest rank in some countries; a U.S. federal or city officer who carries out court orders; head of a fire department; one in charge of a parade.
MARTIAL	Of or suggestive of war; of or connected with military life.

MAT	A flat piece of coarse material used for wiping one's shoes or feet; a decorative border placed around a picture to serve as a contrast between the picture and the frame; *Sports:* - a floor pad to protect athletes, as in wrestling or gymnastics.
MATTE	A dull, often rough finish, as of paint, glass, or paper.

MEAT	The edible flesh of animals, fruits, or vegetables; food; the essence, substance or gist of a thought.
MEET	To come upon; to be introduced to; to be present at an arrival; to join with others, as in a conference. *Sports:* - a contest, especially an athletic competition.

METE — Boundary; *archaic*: measure; to dole; allot.

————————————— ❧ —————————————

METAL — Any of a category of elements that usually have a shiny surface, are generally good conductors of heat and electricity, and can be melted or fused, hammered into thin sheets, or drawn into wire.

METTLE — Courage and fortitude; spirit.

————————————— ❧ —————————————

MEWS — Multiple cries of cats; a narrow street with dwellings converted from stables.

MUSE — To meditate; ponder; ruminate; any of the nine daughters of Zeus, each of whom presided over a different art or science.

————————————— ❧ —————————————

MIGHT — Physical strength, power, force, or influence held by a person or group; used to indicate a condition or state contrary to fact; used to indicate a possibility or probability of the future.

MITE — Various small or minute arthropod animals that are often parasitic on animals and plants.

————————————— ❧ —————————————

MIND — The human consciousness that originates in the brain and is manifested especially in thought, perception, emotion, will, memory, and imagination; to tend, as sheep or children; to obey: *"Mind your manners."*

MINED — To have extracted (ore or minerals) from the earth by digging a tunnel or mine; to have laid explosive mines in a field or avenue of approach by enemy personnel.

lost letters Why do we pronounce **SOLDER** "sodder"??

MINER	One who excavates minerals or ore from a mine; one who places military mines.
MINOR	Lesser or smaller in amount, size, or importance; being under legal age; minor leagues of sports; *Musically*: - a minor key, scale, or interval.

MISSAL	A book containing all that is said or sung at mass during the entire year.
MISSILE	An object or weapon fired or projected at a target.

MISSED	To fail to hit, reach, catch, meet, or otherwise make contact with; to fail to perceive, understand, or experience.
MIST	Fine droplets of a liquid, such as water or perfume.

MOAN	A low, sustained, mournful cry, as of sorrow or pain; a whining complaint.
MOWN	Past participle of MOW, already cut (grass or grain) as with a scythe or machine.

MOAT	A deep, wide ditch, filled with water surrounding a medieval town, fortress, or castle as a defense.
MOTE	A small particle.

MOOSE	A large heavy-antlered mammal of the deer family with humped shoulders and long legs that inhabits northern forested areas.
MOUSSE	Any of various chilled desserts made with flavored whipped cream, gelatin, and eggs.

MUSCLE	A tissue composed of fibers capable of contracting and relaxing to effect bodily movement; strength, power or authority.
MUSSEL	Any of various, especially edible, narrow-shelled marine bivalve mollusks.

NAVAL	Of, relating to, or possessing a navy.
NAVEL	The mark on the abdomen of mammals that marks the point of attachment of fetus and mother.

NAY	No; a denial or refusal.
NEIGH	The long high pitched sound made by a horse.

NIGHT	The period of a day from sunset to sunrise; any period or condition of darkness.
KNIGHT	In the middle ages a military servant of the king or other feudal superior; one, who after serving as a page and squire was formally raised to honorable military rank by the king or other qualified lord.

NONE	No one; nobody; not any; no part.
NUN	A woman who belongs to a religious order.

OAR	A long pole with a blade at one end, used to row or steer a boat.
OR	Used to indicate alternatives, choices, equivalents, and indefiniteness.
ORE	A mineral or rock from which a valuable constituent, especially a metal, can be mined or extracted.

ODE	A lyric poem, often in the form of an address and having an elevated style and formal structure.
OWED	A debt or moral obligation needing to be paid or repaid.

OLEO	Margarine.
OLIO	A mixture; a medley; a miscellany.

ONE	Being a single entity, unit, object, or living being; not two or more; the cardinal number, represented by the symbol 1, designating the first in a series.
WON	The past tense and past participle of WIN.

OWE	To have to pay or repay; to be in debt; to have a moral obligation.
OH	Used to express strong emotion, such as surprise, fear, anger, or pain; also used to indicate understanding.

PAIL	A cylindrical vessel with a handle and sometimes a cover, used for carrying liquids.
PALE	White; pallid; wan, as a pale face or pale blue; lacking intensity or brilliance.

PAIN	The sensations one feels when hurt; suffering or distress of body or mind.
PANE	A piece or division, especially if flat and rectangular; a single division of a window consisting of a piece of glass.

"O" what a difference...

SALON – A large room used for receiving and entertaining guests; a hall or gallery for the exhibition of works of art, or the offering of a product or service related to fashion: *a beauty salon.* But add another "O" and you get **SALOON**, a place where alcoholic drinks are dispensed.

PALL	A covering that darkens or obscures; to lose in interest or attraction.
PAWL	A hinged or pivoted device adapted to fit into a notch of a ratchet wheel to impart forward motion or prevent backward motion.

PAUSE	To cease or suspend an action temporarily, reason for hesitation; *Music:* - a sign indicating that a note or rest is to be held.
PAWS	Plural of PAW. The clawed feet especially of a quadruped animal; human hands; handles clumsily, rudely, or with too much familiarity.

PEACE	Freedom from war or civil strife; law and order.
PIECE	A part or fragment broken or separated from the whole; any single thing, amount, specimen, example; also refers to game components, fire arms and toupees. *Slang:* - a weapon; a pistol or firearm

---

PEAK	A tapering part that projects a pointed end or top, as of a cap, roof, promontory, or mountain; also used to express a high value as to production or performance.
PEEK	To glance or peer quickly and furtively, especially through an opening or from behind something.
PIQUE	A state of vexation caused by a perceived slight; a feeling of wounded pride; to arouse by a provocation or challenge.

PEAL	The loud ringing of a bell or set of matched bells; chimes; or carillon.
PEEL	To strip of skin, bark, or rind; to trim or cut away of any covering.

PEAR	The fleshy fruit of a tree related to the apple.
PAIR	Two things of a kind, similar in form, joined, associated, or used together; two playing cards of the same denomination.

PARE — To remove the outer covering or skin; to peel; to reduce by or as if by cutting off outer parts; to trim: *"The company was forced to pare expenses."*

PEARL — A smooth, lustrous, variously colored deposit formed in the shells of certain mollusks and valued as a gem; highly valued or esteemed.

PURL — To flow or ripple with a murmuring sound as water; an inverted knitting stitch.

PEDAL — A foot operated lever, as on a piano, a bicycle, or an automobile.

PEDDLE — To travel about selling wares.

PEER — An equal; one of the same rank, value or quality. He was judged by a panel of his peers; to look intently, searchingly, or with difficulty.

PIER — A heavy structure supporting the spans of a bridge; a structure built out over water and used as a promenade or a landing place for boats.

PER — To, for, or by each, for every; usage; according to, as *"per the terms of the contract."*

PURR — The soft vibrant sound made by a cat; a sound similar to that made by a cat; *"The engine just purred."*

PHASE	A distinct stage of development; a temporary manner, attitude, or pattern of behavior.
FAZE	To disrupt the composure of, disconcert.

PI	*Mathematics:* - a transcendental number, approximately 3.14159, represents the ratio of the circumference to the diameter of a circle.
PIE	A baked food composed of a shell of pastry that is filled with fruit, meat, cheese, or other ingredients, and usually covered with a pastry crust.

PLAIN	Smooth; level; flat; free from depressions; evident or clear to understand; open; frank; sincere; candid.
PLANE	A tool to make a smooth, level surface; *Boating:* - to rise partly out of the water at high speeds; an airplane.

PLAIT	(can be pronounced plāt or plăt—see next homonym) To braid or to make by braiding, such as hair or ribbon.
PLATE	Sheet metal made by beating, rolling, or casting; a shallow dish, usually circular, from which food is eaten; also the home base in baseball.

PLAT	A small plot of ground; a plan of a piece of land, with actual or proposed features.
PLAIT	(can be pronounced plāt or plăt—see previous homonym) To braid or to make by braiding, such as hair or ribbon.

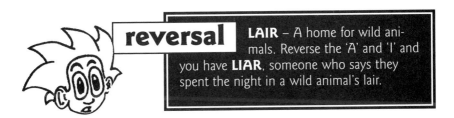

reversal LAIR – A home for wild animals. Reverse the 'A' and 'I' and you have LIAR, someone who says they spent the night in a wild animal's lair.

PLEAS	Plural of PLEA; earnest requests or appeals; *Law:* - the answers of the accused to charges or indictments.
PLEASE	To give enjoyment or satisfaction; to be willing; to like; *Law:* - to be the will or desire of: "*May it please the court.*"

PLUM	A smooth-skinned, fleshy, edible fruit with a hard-shelled pit; an especially desirable position, assignment, or reward.
PLUMB	A weight on the end of a line, used to determine water depth, or to establish true vertical in construction.

POLE	Either end of an axis, especially of the earth; a long rod of any material, as a tent pole or a telephone pole.
POLL	A voting or expression of opinion by individuals; a place where votes are cast and recorded.

PORE	Minute opening, as in an animal's skin or a plant leaf, for the passage of fluid; to read studiously.
POUR	To flow or cause to flow in a steady stream; to rain heavily.

PRIDE	A sense of one's own proper dignity or value; self respect; a company of lions.
PRIED	Past tense and past participle of PRY.

PRAY	To address a prayer to a deity; to make a fervent request for something.
PREY	A victim; an animal hunted or caught for food; to exert an injurious effect.

PRINCE   A male member of the royal family other than the monarch, especially the son of the monarch; the ruler of a principality (originally applied to either sex).

PRINTS   Copies of letters, impressions, photographs, negatives; the end product of a printer.

———————————⌒———————————

PRINCIPAL   First or foremost in importance; chief; the head of an elementary school or high school; a person having a leading or starring role; capitol of financial holdings.

PRINCIPLE   A basic truth, law, or assumption; moral or ethical standards or judgements.

———————————⌒———————————

RAIL   A bar extending horizontally between supports, as in a fence; a steel bar used as a track; to complain bitterly or abusively; a marsh bird having brownish plumage and short wings.

RALE   An abnormal rattling or bubbling sound accompanying the normal breathing, and usually indicating a deceased condition of the lungs or bronchi.

——————————————————————

RAIN   Water condensed from atmospheric vapor and falling in drops.

REIGN   Exercise of sovereign power, as by a Monarch; the period in which a Monarch rules; dominance or widespread influence.

REIN   A long, narrow leather strap attached to each end of the bit of a bridle and used by a rider or driver to control a horse or other animal.

RAISE   To move to a higher position; to erect or build; to cause to exist; to increase in size or worth; to put forward; to arouse or stir up.

RAYS   Thin lines or narrow beams of light or other radiant energy; any of an order of marine fishes having horizontally flattened bodies and narrow tails.

RAZE   To level to the ground.

READ   (Short e) To comprehend the meaning of characters, words, or symbols; to determine the intent or mood of; to obtain information from any and all sources; to perceive an explicit or unexpressed meaning.

RED   Any of a group of colors whose hue resembles that of a ruby; the financial condition of showing a loss: *"in the red."*

READ   (Long e) To get the meaning of language by interpreting its characters or signs: *"what you're doing right now."*

REED   Any of various tall, broad-leaved, related grasses with hollow stems; that which produces a musical tone in an instrument, such as a clarinet.

REAL   Existing or happening as or in fact; actual, true, objectively so; authentic, genuine.

REEL   Any frame or spool on which thread, wire, film, nets, etc. may be wound. It usually turns on an axle, powered by a hand crank or other energy source.

REST   Cessation or absence of work, motion, or activity; a period of inactivity, sleep or quiet activity; something left over, remainder; *Musically:* - an interval of silence having a specified length, and the symbol indicating such a pause.

WREST   To obtain by pulling with violent twisting movements: *"I'm going to wrest the book from his hands."*; to exact by force or persistent effort; wring: "*Wrest the meaning from an obscure poem.*"

RHYME
: Correspondence of terminal sounds of words or of lines of verse; a poem or poems having such correspondence of terminal sounds.

RIME
: Frost or a coating of granular ice, as on grass and trees.

ROAD
: An open, usually public way for the passage of vehicles, people, and animals.

RODE
: The past tense of RIDE.

ROADS
: Plural of ROAD.

RHODES
: The largest of the Dodecanese Islands of S.E. Greece, in the Aegean sea.

ROE
: The eggs of a fish especially while bound together in a mass; a rather small, delicately formed Eurasian deer.

ROW
: To propel a boat with oars; a series of objects or persons placed next to each other, usually in a straight line; a continuous line of buildings along a street.

ROLE
: A character or part played by a performer; a function as to use.

ROLL
: To move or cause to move by repeatedly turning over; to push on wheels or rollers; to move or rock from side to side, as a ship; to wrap something around itself or something else; to make a deep rumbling sound, as thunder; an official list of names.

ROOMER
: A lodger; boarder.

RUMOR
: A report of uncertain origin and accuracy; hearsay.

ROOT	The usually underground portion of a plant that serves as support, draws minerals and water from the soil, and sometimes stores food; a base or support; an essential part; to dig with the snout or nose; to encourage by applause.
ROUTE	A road or way from one place to another; a customary line of travel; a means of reaching a goal.

ROSE	Any of numerous shrubs or vines (or their flowers) of the genus Rosa; the past tense of RISE.
ROWS	The plural of ROW.

ROTE	Memorization through repetition, often without understanding; mechanical routine.
WROTE	The past tense of WRITE.

ROUGH	Having a bumpy or irregular surface, not smooth; coarse or shaggy to the touch; stormy, turbulent; not polished or refined; to prepare or make an unfinished form.
RUFF	A stiffly starched circular collar worn in the 16th and 17th centuries; a fringe of long hair or feathers around the neck of an animal; what Dennis the Menace's dog says!

RUDE	Relatively undeveloped; primitive; crudely or roughly made; ill-mannered; discourteous, abrupt and unpleasant (other than that he was a nice guy).
RUED	Having felt regret, remorse, or sorrow for.

RYE	A widely cultivated cereal grass whose grain is used in making flour; a whisky distilled from a rye mash.
WRY	Dryly humorous; temporarily twisted in an expression of distaste or displeasure.

SALE	The exchange of goods or services for money; a special disposal of goods at lowered prices.
SAIL	A piece of shaped fabric that catches the wind and propels or aids in maneuvering a vessel; to travel by water in a vessel.

SANE	Mentally healthy; reasonable.
SEINE	A large fishing net made to hang vertically in the water by weights and floats.

SAVER	One who avoids waste or expense; one who economizes; one who accumulates money or possessions; One who preserves a person or thing from harm or loss.
SAVOR	The taste or smell of something; a distinctive quality or sensation; to taste with pleasure.

SCENT	Distinctive odor; the trail of a hunted animal or fugitive.
SENT	The past tense and past participle of SEND.
CENT	*Currency*: - one 100th of a dollar, 1/10 of a dime.

SCULL	An oar used for rowing a boat from the stern; one of a pair of short-handled oars used by a single rower; a small light boat for racing.
SKULL	The bony framework of the head; cranium.

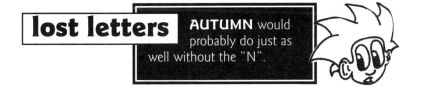

lost letters AUTUMN would probably do just as well without the "N".

SEA	The continuous body of water covering most of the earth's surface; a large body of water completely or partially enclosed by land.
SEE	To perceive with the eye; to regard; to understand; to believe possible; to meet; to foresee; to visit socially; to make sure; the seat of jurisdiction of a bishop.

———————————— ℮ ————————————

SEAM	A line formed by sewing together two pieces of material; a thin layer of stratum, as of coal.
SEEM	To give the impression of being; to appear to be.

———————————— ℮ ————————————

SEAMEN	The plural of SEAMAN (sailors).
SEMEN	A whitish secretion of the male reproduction tract, containing sperm.

———————————— ℮ ————————————

SEED	A ripened ovule of a flowering plant that may develop into a new plant; to plant; to deteriorate: *"going to seed."*
CEDE	To surrender possession of, especially by treaty; to yield or grant.

———————————— ℮ ————————————

SELL	To exchange for money or its equivalent; to promote successfully; to convince.
CELL	A narrow confining room, as in a prison or convent; a small enclosed space, as in a honeycomb; the smallest structural unit of an organism.

———————————— ℮ ————————————

SERF	A member of a servile class bound to the land and subject to the will of the landowner; slave.
SURF	The waves of the sea as they break upon a shore or reef.

———————————— ℮ ————————————

SEW	To make, repair, or fasten by stitching, as with a needle and thread.
SOW	To plant seeds to produce a crop; to propagate or disseminate.

SO	In a manner expressed or indicated; "Hold the brush so."; apparently; in truth; expression of surprise or comprehension; fifth note on the music scale.

SEWER	An artificial, underground conduit for carrying off liquid waste or rainwater.
SUER	One who institutes legal proceedings to redress grievances; one who makes an appeal.

SHEAR	To remove (fleece or hair) by cutting or clipping; to divest or deprive.
SHEER	Thin and transparent, as curtains; undiluted, pure; almost perpendicular, steep.

SHOE	A durable covering for the feet.
SHOO	Word used to frighten away pests: "*Shoo, fly!*"

SHONE	Past tense and past participle of SHINE.
SHOWN	Caused or allowed to be seen; displayed; *Racing:* - having finished third.

SIC	Intentionally so written - used after a printed word or passage to indicate that it exactly reproduces an original; also to set upon, attack.
SICK	Suffering from a physical or mental illness; defective; weary; insane: "*a 'sick' person.*"

pun-ishment   What's a moocher's sweet treat??

SPONGE CAKE!!

SIGHT   The power of seeing; a view; something worth seeing; a device used to assist aim by guiding the eye, as
on a firearm.

SITE   A place where something was, is, or is to be located.

CITE   To quote as an authority or example; to mention as
support, illustration, or proof; to commend officially
or militarily.

———————————————— ℮ ————————————————

SIOUX   A member of a group of Native Americans of the
Great Plains, mainly in North and South Dakota.

SUE   To institute legal proceedings to redress grievances;
to make an appeal.

———————————————— ℮ ————————————————

SLAY   To kill.

SLEIGH   A light vehicle on runners for travel or fun on snow
or ice.

———————————————— ℮ ————————————————

SLIGHT   Small in size, degree, or amount; frail; of small
importance; an act of deliberate discourtesy or disre-
spect.

SLEIGHT   Trickery; dexterity; *"sleight of hand."*

———————————————— ℮ ————————————————

SLOE   The tart, blue-black, plumlike fruit of the black-
thorn.

SLOW   Not moving or able to move quickly; taking or
requiring a long time; not having or showing mental
quickness.

———————————————— ℮ ————————————————

SOAR   To rise, fly, or glide high in the air; to climb swiftly
or powerfully.

SORE   Painful or tender; feeling pain; an open skin lesion,
wound, or ulcer.

———————————————— ℮ ————————————————

SOLE   The underside of the foot, shoe, or boot, excluding
the heel; *Sports:* - the bottom surface of the head of

	golf club; of or relating to only one individual or group; any of various marine flatfish related to and resembling the flounder.
SOUL	An entity which is regarded as being the immortal or spiritual part of a person, though having no physical or material reality.

⁕

SPADE	A digging tool with a long handle and a flat blade; one of four suits in playing cards.
SPAYED	Having removed the ovaries of an animal.

⁕

STAIRS	A flight of steps; a staircase.
STARES	Looks directly and fixedly, often with a wide-eyed gaze.

⁕

STAKE	A pointed piece of wood or metal driven into the ground as a marker, barrier, or support; a post to which an offender is bound for execution by burning; money or property risked in a wager; share or interest in an enterprise.
STEAK	A slice or slab of meat, usually beef, grilled or broiled.

⁕

STATIONARY	Not moving, or not capable of being moved; fixed; "*A stationary sound.*"
STATIONERY	Writing paper, envelopes, writing materials and office supplies.

⁕

STEAL	To take the property of another without permission; to move, carry, or place stealthily; *Baseball:* - to advance a base safely during the delivery of a pitch.
STEEL	A hard, durable, strong, malleable alloy of iron and carbon.

STRAIGHT   Extending continuously, horizontally or vertically, in the same direction without curving; honesty; fair-minded; not deviating from what is considered socially normal or acceptable; five sequential cards in poker.

STRAIT   A narrow channel joining two larger bodies of water.

STYLE   A way in which something is said, done, expressed, or performed; of customary manner; to make consistent with rules; to arrange or design.

STILE   A set or series of steps for crossing a fence or wall.

SUM   The result obtained by addition, as to quantity, numbers, money, or thoughts.

SOME   Being an unspecified number or quantity; unknown or unspecified by name.

SUN   The incandescent body of gasses about which the earth and other planets revolve and which furnishes light, heat, and energy for the solar system; the star nearest the earth.

SON   A male child in relation to his parents or parent; any male descendant.

SUNDAE   A dish of ice cream with any of various toppings such as syrup, fruits, nuts, and whipped cream.

SUNDAY   The first day of the week; the sabbath for many Christians.

SWEET   Having the taste of sugar; pleasing to the senses, mind, or feelings; a dear or beloved person.

SUITE   A series of connected rooms used as a unit; *Musically:* - an instrumental composition consisting of a succession of short pieces, as of material drawn from a longer work.

SYMBOL	Something that represents something by association, resemblance, or conviction, especially a material object used to represent something invisible; a printed or written sign used to represent an operation, an element, a quantity, a quality, or a relation, as in mathematics or music.
CYMBAL	*Music:* - a concave brass plate that produces a brilliant clashing sound, generally used in pairs.

TACKED	Loosely stitched or otherwise temporarily attached; *Sailing:* - adjusted course relative to the wind.
TACT	Sensitivity in dealing with others.

TACKS	Short light nails with sharp points and a flat heads.
TAX	A contribution for the support of a government required of persons, groups, or businesses within the domain of that government; an excessive demand.

TAIL   The rear end or a process extending from the rear end of an animal; the rear end of a vehicle, aircraft, bomb, missile, or kite; the side of a coin not having the principal design or date; *Informal:* - the act of following a person or animal on the move.

TALE   A recital of events or happenings; a narrative of imaginary happenings; a lie.

TAPER	A slender candle or waxed wick; a gradual decrease in thickness or width of an elongated object; to make or become gradually narrower or thinner toward one end.
TAPIR	A tropical American or Asian mammal with a heavy body, short legs, and a long fleshy upper lip.

TARE	(tăr) A deduction from gross weight made to allow for the weight of the container.
TEAR	(tăr) To pull apart or into pieces; to make an opening by ripping; to separate forcefully.

TAUGHT	The past tense and past participle of TEACH; "*You can be taught if you allow someone to teach.*"
TAUT	Tight; not slack; strained.

TEA	Dried processed leaves of an Asian shrub, steeped in boiling water to make a beverage.
TEE	A small peg with a concave top for holding a golf ball for an initial drive; the area of each golf hole from which the initial drive is made.

TEAM	A group on the same side, as in a game or work group; two or more draft animals harnessed to the same vehicle or implement.
TEEM	To abound or swarm; to become filled to overflowing.

TEAR	(tĭr) A drop of clear salty liquid that lubricates the surface between the eyeball and eyelid; the act of weeping.
TIER	(tĭr) One of two or more rows arranged one above another.

how about this... PORT - - Could be a wine or a sailors' destination.

TEAS	The plural of TEA; a rather formal social gathering, held mid-afternoon.
TEASE	To annoy, make fun of; to arouse hope, desire, or curiosity without affording satisfaction; to brush or comb hair toward the scalp.

_____ ℮ _____

TENSE	Tightly stretched; feeling mental or nervous tension; any of the inflected forms of a verb that indicate the time and continuance or completion of the action or state.
TENTS	The plural of TENT (portable living quarters).

_____ ℮ _____

THEIR	The possessive form of they.
THERE	At or in that place; at the stage, moment, or point.
THEY'RE	A contraction of the words "they are."

_____ ℮ _____

THREW	Past tense of THROW. Propelled through the air with a swift motion of the hand or arm.
THROUGH	In one side and out the other; from beginning to end; finished with; concluded.

_____ ℮ _____

THRONE	A chair occupied by a sovereign or bishop.
THROWN	Past participle of THROW.

_____ ℮ _____

TIC	A habitual spasmodic muscular twitching of muscles especially of the face.
TICK	A light, sharp, clicking sound made repeatedly by a machine, such as a clock; any of numerous small blood-sucking parasitic arachnids many of which transmit diseases; a light mattress without inner springs, or a cloth case for a regular mattress or pillow; the repetitious sound of a clock.

TIDE	A periodic variation in the surface level of the oceans, bays, gulfs, inlets, and estuaries, caused by the gravitational attraction of the moon and sun; to support through a difficult period; *"I asked for $100 to tide me over till payday."*; the brand name of a popular laundry detergent.
TIED	Fastened or secured with a cord, rope, strap, or laces; confined or restricted; brought together in a relationship; connected or united; equaled an opponent's score in a contest.

TIMBER	Trees or wooded land considered as a source of wood; wood used as a building material; a structural beam.
TIMBRE	A sound's quality which distinguishes it from others of the same pitch and volume.

TO	In a direction toward; as far as; reaching a given state; in contact with; in a relation with; compared with; so that.
TOO	In addition; also: excessively.
TWO	The cardinal number equal to the sum of 1 + 1; the 2nd in a set of sequence.

TON	A measure of weight: (a short ton is 2,000 lbs., a long ton is 2,240 lbs).
TUN	A large cask.

TRAY	A shallow flat receptacle with a raised edge, used for carrying, holding or displaying articles.
TREY	A card or die with three (3) pips.

TURN	To move or cause to move around an axis or center; to rotate or revolve; to change direction; to become sour or change color; to change for the better.

| TERN | Any of various sea birds resembling gulls, usually smaller and having a forked tail. |

| VALE | A valley, dale. |
| VEIL | Something that conceals or obscures; a length of sheer cloth worn over the head, shoulders, and often the face; the life or vows of a nun. |

VANE	A weather vane; a metal guidance or stabilizing fin attached to the tail of a bomb or other missile.
VEIN	A vessel through which the blood returns to the heart; one of the branching structures forming the framework of a leaf or an insects wing; a long, regularly shaped deposit of ore; lode.
VAIN	Excessively proud of one's appearance or accomplishment; conceited; not successful: *"It was a vain attempt."*

| VIAL | A small container for liquids. |
| VILE | Loathsome, disgusting; unpleasant or objectionable; miserably poor; morally low. |

| VICE | An evil, degrading, or immoral practice or habit. |
| VISE | A clamping device of metal or wood, usually consisting of two jaws used to hold a piece in position. |

| WAIL | To cry loudly or mournfully, as in grief or protest. |
| WHALE | Any of an order of often very large marine mammals having flippers, a tail with horizontal flukes, and one or two blow holes for breathing; to thrash or strike vigorously. |

WAIST	The bottom of the human trunk between the bottom of the rib cage and the pelvis.
WASTE	To use, consume, or expend thoughtlessly or carelessly; to lose or cause to lose energy, strength, or vigor; to fail to take advantage of; refuse, as garbage.

℮

WAIT	To remain in expectation; to be ready for use; the act of, or time spent waiting.
WEIGHT	A measure of the heaviness of an object; overpowering force.

℮

WARE	Articles of the same general kind; hardware, silverware.
WEAR	To use as an article of clothing; to impair or decay by use or by scraping or rubbing.

℮

WARN	To make aware of present or potential danger; caution; to admonish as to action or manners; to notify to go or stay away; to notify or apprise in advance.
WORN	Past participle of WEAR; affected or impaired by wear or use; showing the wearing effects of overwork or suffering.

℮

WAVE	To move or cause to move up or down, or back and forth in the air; to move or swing as in giving a signal; to curve or curl as hair.
WAIVE	To give up (a claim or right) voluntarily; to postpone.

℮

WAY	A road, route, path, or passage that leads from one place to another; space to proceed; a course of action or state of affairs; progress or advancement in accomplishing a goal.
WEIGH	To determine the weight of by or as if by using a scale or balance; to consider or balance in the mind; to ponder.

WEAK	Lacking physical strength, energy, or vigor; feeble; likely to fail under pressure, stress, or strain; unable to function normally or fully.
WEEK	A period of seven days, especially a period that begins on a Sunday and continues through the next Saturday, usually devoted to periods of work, school, or business.

WINED	Past tense of wine: - "*Wined and dined.*"
WIND	(Long i) To wrap (something) around the center of another object once or repeatedly; to turn (a crank, for example) in a series of circular motions; to coil the spring of (a mechanism) by turning a stem or cord: "*wind a watch.*"

WOOD	The tough fibrous supporting and water-conducting tissue beneath the bark of trees and shrubs, consisting largely of cellulose and lignin.
WOULD	Past tense of WILL.

WRAP	To draw, fold, or wind about in order to cover; to enclose within a covering.
RAP	To hit sharply or swiftly; a prison sentence; *Slang:* - a talk, a spoken or chanted rhyming lyric with a rhythmic accompaniment.

WRAPPED	Past tense and past participle of WRAP; to cover, envelop, or encase; to clasp, fold, or coil.
RAPT	Deeply moved, absorbed, or delighted; enraptured.

lost letters Has anyone ever heard the "P" in **PSALM**??

WRAPPER	That in which an object is wrapped or covered; one that wraps, as a store employee who wraps parcels.
RAPPER	One that raps or strikes, especially a door knocker; *Music:* - one who performs rap.

―――――――――――――――――e――

WRITE	To form or inscribe (words, letters, symbols, etc.) on a surface, as by cutting, carving; marking with a pen or pencil; to communicate via the written word.
RIGHT	Not curved; straight, as a line or plane; correct in thought, statement, or action; fitting; appropriate; suitable; most convenient or favorable; direction to the side of the body away from the heart.

―――――――――――――――――e――

WRING	To twist or squeeze, especially to extract water; to twist together as a sign of anguish.
RING	A circular band, often of precious metal, worn on the finger; an enclosed area in which exhibitions or contests take place; a group of people acting to advance their interests; to sound resonantly when struck.

―――――――――――――――――e――

YOKE	A crossbar with two U-shaped pieces that encircle the necks of draft animals.
YOLK	The yellow portion of the egg of a bird or reptile.

―――――――――――――――――e――

YOU	The one or ones being addressed.
YEW	A poisonous evergreen tree or shrub having scarlet cup-shaped seeds and flat, dark green needles.
EWE	A female sheep.

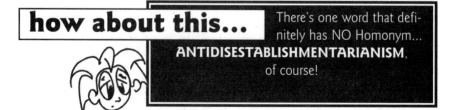

how about this... There's one word that definitely has NO Homonym...
ANTIDISESTABLISHMENTARIANISM,
of course!

Homonyms "C"

These are words which are spelled the same, but have
different pronunciations and different meanings!

BASS   (băs) Any of numerous sport and food bony fishes,
such as sea bass and striped bass.

(bās) A low-pitched tone or sound; the lowest part in
vocal or instrumental music; a male singing voice of
the lowest range, as well as the singer who has such a
voice.

CLOSE   (klōs) Being near in space, time, relationships, mutual
interests, loyalties, or affections; having little or no

space between ele-
ments or parts;
tight and compact;
being near the
surface, on the
brink of, decided
by a narrow mar-
gin, or faithful to
the original.

(klōz) To move (a
door, for example)
so that an opening or passage is covered or obstruct-
ed; shut; to bar access to; to fill or stop up; to stop
the operations of; to bring to an end, such as negoti-
ations; to join, unite, draw, or bind together.

CONVICT   (con–**vict**) To find or prove (someone) guilty of an
offense or crime, especially by the verdict of a court.

(**con**–vict) A person found or declared guilty of an
offense or crime; a person serving a sentence of
imprisonment.

DEFECT   (dē–fect) The lack of something necessary or desirable for completion or perfection; deficiency: *"The material was on sale because of a defect."*

                (de–fĕct) To disown allegiance to one's country and take up residence in another; to abandon a position or association, often to join an opposing group: *"He defected from the party over the issue of free trade."*

DESERT   (dĕz–ert) A barren or desolate area; dry, often sandy with little rainfall, extreme temperatures, and sparse vegetation.

                (dĕ–zert) To leave empty or alone; to abandon.

DOVE   (dŭv) Any of numerous pigeons, having a characteristic cooing call; a gentle person or one who advocates peace.

                (dōv) The past tense of DIVE.

ENTRANCE (ĕn–trens) A means or place of entry; the act of entering.

                (ĕn–trăns) To fill with delight, wonder or enchantment.

EXCUSE   (ĕk–**skyooz**) To grant pardon to; forgive; to give per-
           mission to leave; release: *"The child ate quickly and
           asked to be excused."*

           (ĕk–**skyūs**) An explanation offered to justify or obtain
           forgiveness; a reason or grounds for excusing:
           "Ignorance is no excuse for breaking the law."

INCENSE   (in–**sens**) To cause to be extremely angry; infuriate.

           (**in**–sens) An aromatic substance, such as wood or a
           gum, that is burned to produce a pleasant odor.

INTIMATE   (**in**–ti–**mit**) Marked by close acquaintance, associa-
           tion, or familiarity.

           (**in**–ti–**māt**) To make known subtly and indirectly; to
           hint.

INVALID   (**in**–va–lid) One who is incapacitated by a chronic ill-
           ness or disability.

           (in–**văl**–id) Not legally or factually valid; falsely based
           or reasoned.

LEAD   (lēd) To show the way to by going in advance; to
           guide, direct, or go first.

           (lĕd) A soft, malleable, ductile, bluish-white, dense
           metallic element, extracted chiefly from galena.

MINUTE   (**min**–ut) A unit of time equal to one sixtieth of an
           hour, 60 seconds.

           (my–**nūt**) Exceptionally small; tiny; insignificant.

MODERATE (mŏ–der–ĭt) Being within reasonable limits, not excessive or extreme; a moderate price; a moderate climate.

(mŏ–der–āt) To preside over: "*She was chosen to moderate the convention.*"

OBJECT (ŏb–jĕkt) Something perceptable to one's senses, a material thing; a focus; the object of contempt, or a purpose, aim, or goal: the object of the game.

(ŏb–jĕkt) To present a dissenting or opposing argument, raise an objection: objected to the testimony of the witness; to express disapproval of something.

OVERAGE (ō–ver–ĭj) An amount, as of money or goods, that exceeds the listed amount in records or books; a surplus; an excess.

(ō–ver–āj) Older than usual for a particular position or activity.

POLISH (pō–lish) Of or relating to Poland or its people, their language, or culture.

(pŏl–ish) To make smooth and shiny by rubbing or chemical reaction: she polished the silverware; to remove flaws from; perfect or complete; "*She needs to polish her piano technique.*"

PRESENT (prĕs–ent) A moment or period in time perceptible as intermediate between past and future; now; a gift.

(prĭ–zent) To introduce with formal or informal ceremony; the guest speaker was presented to the audience.

READ   (rēd) To examine, grasp, or render aloud, the meaning of written or printed characters, words, or sentences.

(rĕd) Something that has been studied or learned by reading; informed by reading; learned.

REBEL   (re–**bĕl**) To resist the authority of one's government; to feel or express strong unwillingness or repugnance; she rebelled at the sight of blood.

(**rĕb**–el) One who rebels or is in rebellion, often used to modify another noun: rebel troops; a rebel army.

RECORD   (re–**kord**) To set down for preservation in writing or other permanent form; to register the words, sound, appearance, or performance in permanent form by mechanical or electrical means for reproduction.

(**rĕk**–erd) An account, as of information or facts, set down especially in writing as a means of preserving knowledge. Also a disk designed to be played on a phonograph, or a tape on which sound and/or visual images have been recorded.

REFUSE   (re–**fyūz**) To decline to do, accept, give, or allow.

(**ref**–yoos) Anything discarded or rejected as useless or worthless; trash.

wild A's Looking for the words that have alternate "A's" from Page 56?

PAPAYA and **CATAMARAN**

ROW   (rō) A series of objects placed next to each other, usually in a straight line; *Nautical:* - to propel (a boat) with or as if with oars.

(rou) A boisterous disturbance or quarrel; a brawl.

SAKE   (sāk) For personal benefit, motive, interest, or welfare.

(să–kee) A Japanese alcoholic beverage made from fermented rice.

SEWER   (sū–er) An artificial conduit for carrying of sewage or rainwater.

(sō–er) One who sews.

SHOWER (shou–er) A brief fall of rain, hail, or sleet; a party held to honor and present gifts to someone; a bath taken with sprayed water.

(shō–er) One that shows or presents for viewing.

SINGER (sing–er) *Music:* - One who sings, a trained or professional vocalist.

(sin–jer) One who singes (burns with a flame).

SLAVER (slă–ver) To slobber; drool.

(slā–ver) A person or ship, that is engaged in the trafficking of slaves.

SOW   (sō) To scatter (seed) over the ground for growing.

(sou) The adult female of several animals, such as the hog and the bear.

SUBJECT   (**sub**–<u>jikt</u>) Being in a position or in circumstances that place one under the power or authority of another or others: *"All citizens in this nation are subject to the law."*

(sub–**jekt**) To submit for consideration; to submit to the authority of; to expose to something: *"The patients on the ward were subjected to infection."*

TEAR   (t<u>ĕ</u>r) To pull apart or into pieces by force; rend.

(t<u>ĭ</u>r) A drop of clear salty liquid that is secreted by the eye to lubricate the eyeball and eyelid and to wash away irritants; to cry tears.

TOWER   (**tou**-wer) A build-ing or part of a building that is exceptionally high in proportion to its width and length.

(t<u>ō</u>-er) Someone or something that tows, such as a sled, a car, or a barge.

USE   (yoo<u>z</u>) To put into practice or apply for a purpose: employ; to avail oneself of; practice: use caution.

(yoo<u>s</u>) The act of using; the application or employ-ment of something for a purpose: with the use of a calculator; skilled in the use of the bow and arrow.

WICKED   (**wĭk**–ĕd) Evil by nature and in practice; playfully malicious or mischievous: a wicked prank; severe: "*a wicked cough*"; offensive; *Slang*: - strikingly good, effective, or skillful: a wicked curve ball.

               (wĭkt) Conveyed by capillary action: absorbent cloth that wicks moisture away from the skin.

WIND   (wĭnd) Moving air, especially a natural and perceptible movement of air parallel to or along the ground.

               (wīnd) To wrap (something) around a center of another object once or repeatedly; to turn (a crank, for example) in a series of circular motions.

WOUND   (woond) An injury, especially one in which the skin or other external surface is torn, pierced, cut, or otherwise broken.

               (wound) The past tense and past participle of WIND (long i).

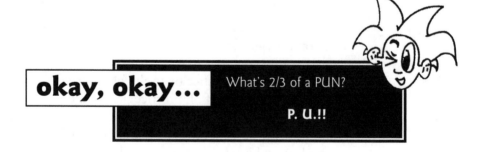

okay, okay...   What's 2/3 of a PUN?

P. U.!!

~The End~

P.S. This is just to add to your confusion. Most dictionaries list three groups in the overall "HOMONYM" category. They are:

1. HOMONYM (This is our Group "A"): One of two or more words that have the same sound and often the same spelling, but differ in meaning. Also, a word that is used to designate several different things.

2. HOMOPHONE (This is our Group "B"): One of two or more words, such as *night* and *knight*, that are pronounced the same, but differ in meaning, origin, and sometimes spelling.

3. HOMOGRAPH (This is our Group "C"): One of two or more words that have the same spelling, but differ in origin, meaning, and sometimes pronunciation.

P.P.S. We deliberately put these descriptions way back here so as not to *muddy the waters*, so to speak, before you dug into the book's contents.

~ATTENTION~

No doubt, we have missed many possible inclusions in this, our first printing. If there is something we've missed that you would like to see included in the next edition of *HOMONYMS–Why English Suffers*, please drop us a line!

_____

_____

_____

_____

_____

_____

_____

_____

Send your submissions to:

Barbed Wire Publishing
270 Avenida de Mesilla
Las Cruces, NM 88005
thefolks@barbed-wire.net

Thanks, and we hope you've had some fun!

~NOTES~

~NOTES~

~INDEX~

This index is an alphabetical listing of all the words presented in this book. Each entry directs the reader to the section in which that entry appears and is defined. The sections are:

HOMONYMS "A" (pages 1-51) – Words which have the same spelling and pronunciation, but different definitions;

HOMONYMS "B" (pages 53-106) – Words which have the same pronunciation, but different spellings and definitions; and

HOMONYMS "C" (pages 107-114) – Words which are spelled the same, but have different pronunciations and different meanings!

Boer . . . . .B	Canter . . . . .B	Coax . . . . .B
Bole . . . . .B	Cantor . . . . .B	Cob . . . . .A
Boll . . . . .B	Cape . . . . .A	Cokes . . . . .B
Border . . . . .B	Caper . . . . .A	Colonel . . . . .B
Bore . . . . .B	Capital . . . . .B	Comb . . . . .A
Bored . . . . .B	Capitol . . . . .B	Convict C
Bound . . . . .A	Carat . . . . .B	Coop . . . . .B
Bow . . . . .B	Carrot . . . . .B	Coral . . . . .B
Bowl . . . . .B	Cart . . . . .B	Cord . . . . .B
Boy . . . . .B	Case . . . . .A	Core . . . . .B
Brake . . . . .B	Cash . . . . .B	Corps . . . . .B
Bread . . . . .B	Cast . . . . .B	Corral . . . . .B
Break . . . . .B	Caste . . . . .B	Council . . . . .B
Bred . . . . .B	Cede . . . . .B	Counsel . . . . . . .B
Bridal . . . . .B	Ceiling . . . . .B	Counter . . . . . . .A
Bridge . . . . .A	Cell . . . . .B	Coupe . . . . .B
Bridle . . . . .B	Cellar . . . . .B	Course . . . . .B
Broach . . . . .B	Cent . . . . .B	Court . . . . .A
Brooch . . . . .B	Cents . . . . .B	Creak . . . . .B
Brush . . . . .A	Cereal . . . . .B	Creek . . . . .B
Buoy . . . . .B	Certain . . . . .A	Crop . . . . .A
Burro . . . . .B	Chase . . . . .A	Cue . . . . .B
Burrow . . . . .B	Chased . . . . .B	Currant . . . . .B
Bus . . . . .B	Chaste . . . . .B	Current . . . . .B
Buss . . . . .B	Cheap . . . . .B	Cymbal . . . . .B
But . . . . .B	Cheep . . . . . .B & C	
Butt . . . . .B	Chews . . . . .B	**D**
Buy . . . . .B	Choir . . . . .B	
By . . . . .B	Choose . . . . .B	Dam . . . . .B
Bye . . . . .B	Choral . . . . .B	Damn . . . . .B
Byte . . . . .B	Chorale . . . . .B	Darn . . . . .A
	Chord . . . . .B	Dash . . . . .A
C	Chute . . . . .B	Date . . . . .A
	Cite . . . . .B	Dear . . . . .B
Cache . . . . .B	Clause . . . . .B	Deck . . . . .A
Calf . . . . .A	Claws . . . . .B	Decline . . . . .A
Camp . . . . .A	Close C	Deed . . . . .A
Can . . . . .A	Coarse . . . . .B	Deer . . . . .B

Defect C
Desert ......B & C
Dessert ....B
Dew ....B
Die ....B
Dive ....A
Do ....B
Doc ....B
Dock ....B
Doe ....B
Done ....B
Dough ....B
Dove C
Down ....A
Drill ....A
Drone ....A
Duck ....A
Dual ....B
Due ....B
Duel ....B
Dun ....B
Dye ....B

E

Ear ....A
Earn ....B
Eave ....B
Eerie ....B
Eight ....B
El ....B
Ell ....B
Entrance C
Erie ....B
Eve ....B
Ewe ....B
Excuse C
Eye ....B

F

Facts ....B
Faint ....B
Fair ....B
Fairy ....B
Fan ....A
Faker ....B
Fakir ....B
Fare ....B
Fast ....A
Fathom ....A
Fawn ....A
Fax ....B
Faze ....B
Feat ....B
Feet ....B
Feint ....B
Felt ....A
Ferry ....B
Fete ....B
Few ....B
File ....A
Fin ....A
Fine ....A
Fir ....B
Firm ....A
Fit ....A
Flag ....A
Flair ....B
Flare ....B
Flat ....A
Flatter ....A
Flea ....B
Flee ....B
Fleet ....A
Flew ....B
Flight ....A

Floc ....B
Flock ....B
Floe ....B
Flour ....B
Flow ....B
Flower ....B
Flu ....B
Flue ....B
Flush ....A
Fly ....A
Foil ....A
Fold ....A
Font ....A
For ....B
Fore ....B
Foreword ....B
Forge ....A
Forth ....B
Found ....A
Founder ....A
Fourth ....B
Forward ....B
Foul ....B
Four ....B
Fowl ....B
Frees ....B
Freeze ....B
Fret ....A
Friar ....B
Fry ....A
Fryer ....B
Fur ....B
Fuse ....A
Fuzz ....A

G

Gael ....B

Gait ....B	Hanger ....B	Hour ....B
Gale ....B	Hare ....B	Husky ....A
Gall ....B	Hart ....B	Hymn ....B
Game ....A	Hatch ....A	
Gate ....B	Haul ....B	**I**
Gaul ....B	Hawk ....A	
Gee ....A	Hay ....B	Idle ....B
Gibe ....A	Haze ....A	Idol ....B
Gild ....B	Heal ....B	Incense C
Gnu ....B	Hear ....B	Intimate C
Gofer ....B	Heard ....B	Invalid C
Gopher ....B	Heart ....B	Isle ....B
Gorge ....A	Heel ....B	
Graft ....A	Heir ....B	**J**
Grate ....B	Herd ....B	
Grave ....A	Here ....B	Jam ....B
Graze ....A	Heroin ....B	Jamb ....B
Great ....B	Heroine ....B	Jar ....A
Grill ....A	Hey ....B	Jerk ....A
Grip ....A	Hi ....B	Junk ....A
Guessed ....B	Hide ....A	
Guest ....B	Hie ....B	**K**
Guild ....B	High ....B	
Guise ....B	Higher ....B	Karat ....B
Guy ....A	Him ....B	Kart ....B
Guys ....B	Hip ....A	Kernel ....B
Gyro ....A	Hire ....B	Key ....A
	Hoard ....B	Kind ....A
H	Hoarse ....B	Kitty ....A
	Hold ....A	Knead ....B
Habit ....A	Hole ....B	Knee ....B
Hack ....A	Holey ....B	Kneed ....B
Hail ....B	Holy ....B	Knew ....B
Hair ....B	Hood ....A	Knight ....B
Hale ....B	Horde ....B	Knot ....B
Hall ....B	Horse ....B	Know ....B
Hamper ....A	Hose ....A	Knows ....B
Hangar ....B	Host ....A	

L

Lade . . . . .B
Laid . . . . .B
Lain . . . . .B
Lam . . . . .B
Lama . . . . .B
Lamb . . . . .B
Lane . . . . .B
Lap . . . . .A
Lark . . . . .A
Lash . . . . .A
Last . . . . .A
Launch . . . . .A
Lay . . . . .B
Lead . . . . . . .B & C
League . . . . .A
Leak . . . . .B
Lean . . . . .B
Leaves . . . . .A
Led . . . . .B
Leech . . . . .A
Leek . . . . .B
Left . . . . .A
Lei . . . . .B
Let . . . . .A
Levee . . . . .B
Levy . . . . .B
Liar . . . . .B
Lie . . . . .B
Lien . . . . .B
Light . . . . .A
Like . . . . .A
Lime . . . . .A
Line . . . . .A
List . . . . .A
Litter . . . . .A
Llama . . . . .B

Load . . . . .B
Loaf . . . . .A
Lock . . . . .A
Locks . . . . .B
Lode . . . . .B
Lodge . . . . .A
Log . . . . .A
Long . . . . .A
Loom . . . . .A
Loot . . . . .B
Lox . . . . .B
Lumber . . . . . . .A
Lush . . . . .A
Lute . . . . .B
Lye . . . . .B
Lyre . . . . .B

M

Mach . . . . .B
Made . . . . .B
Maid . . . . .B
Mail . . . . .B
Main . . . . .B
Maize . . . . .B
Male . . . . .B
Mall . . . . .B
Mane . . . . .B
Mantel . . . . .B
Mantle . . . . .B
March . . . . .A
Maroon . . . . .A
Marshal . . . . .B
Martial . . . . .B
Mat . . . . .B
Match . . . . .A
Matte . . . . .B
Maul . . . . .B

May . . . . .A
Maze . . . . .B
Meal . . . . .A
Mean . . . . .A
Meat . . . . .B
Meet . . . . .B
Meld . . . . .A
Metal . . . . .B
Mete . . . . .B
Meter . . . . .A
Mettle . . . . .B
Mews . . . . .B
Might . . . . .B
Mind . . . . .B
Mine . . . . .A
Mined . . . . .B
Miner . . . . .B
Minor . . . . .B
Mint . . . . .A
Minute C
Miss . . . . .A
Missal . . . . .B
Missed . . . . .B
Missile . . . . .B
Mist . . . . .B
Mite . . . . .B
Moan . . . . .B
Moat . . . . .B
Mock . . . . .B
Moderate C
Mold . . . . .A
Mole . . . . .A
Moose . . . . .B
Mote . . . . .B
Mousse . . . . .B
Mown . . . . .B
Muff . . . . .A
Mug . . . . .A

Mule . . . . .A
Muscle . . . . .B
Muse . . . . .B
Mush . . . . .A
Mussel . . . . .B
Muzzle . . . . .A

N

Nag . . . . .A
Nail . . . . .A
Nap . . . . .A
Naval . . . . .B
Navel . . . . .B
Nay . . . . .B
Nee . . . . .B
Need . . . . .B
Neigh . . . . .B
Net . . . . .A
New . . . . .B
Night . . . . .B
Nip . . . . .A
No . . . . .B
Noes . . . . .B
None . . . . .B
Noodle . . . . .A
Nose . . . . .B
Not . . . . .B
Novel . . . . .A
Nun . . . . .B

O

Oar . . . . .B
Object C
Ode . . . . .B
Oh . . . . .B
Oleo . . . . .B

Olio . . . . .B
One . . . . .B
Ooze . . . . .A
Operate . . . . .A
Or . . . . .B
Ore . . . . .B
Organ . . . . .A
Our . . . . .B
Overage C
Owe . . . . .B
Owed . . . . .B
Own . . . . .A

P

Pad . . . . .A
Paddle . . . . .A
Page . . . . .A
Pail . . . . .B
Pain . . . . .B
Pair . . . . .B
Pale . . . . .B
Pall . . . . .B
Palm . . . . .A
Pan . . . . .A
Pane . . . . .B
Panhandle . . . . . . .A
Pare . . . . .B
Pat . . . . .A
Pause . . . . .B
Paw . . . . .A
Pawl . . . . .B
Pawn . . . . .A
Paws . . . . .B
Peace . . . . .B
Peak . . . . .B
Peal . . . . .B
Pear . . . . .B

Pearl . . . . .B
Peck . . . . .A
Pedal . . . . .B
Peddle . . . . .B
Peek . . . . .B
Peel . . . . .B
Peep . . . . .A
Peer . . . . .B
Pelt . . . . .A
Pen . . . . .A
Per . . . . .B
Perch . . . . .A
Perk . . . . .A
Phase . . . . .B
Phew . . . . .B
Pi . . . . .B
Pick . . . . .A
Pie . . . . .B
Piece . . . . .B
Pier . . . . .B
Pike . . . . .A
Pile . . . . .A
Pine . . . . .A
Pique . . . . .B
Pit . . . . .A
Pitch . . . . .A
Pitcher . . . . .A
Plain . . . . .B
Plait . . . . .B
Plane . . . . .B
Plaque . . . . .A
Plat . . . . .B
Plate . . . . .B
Pleas . . . . .B
Please . . . . .B
Plum . . . . .B
Plumb . . . . .B
Poach . . . . .A

Pod . . . . .A
Poker . . . . .A
Pole . . . . .B
Policy . . . . .A
Polish C
Poll . . . . .B
Pool . . . . .A
Poop . . . . .A
Pop . . . . .A
Pore . . . . .B
Port . . . . .A
Pose . . . . .A
Post . . . . .A
Pot . . . . .A
Pound . . . . .A
Pour . . . . .B
Pray . . . . .B
Prayer . . . . .A
Present C
Prey . . . . .B
Pride . . . . .B
Pried . . . . .B
Primer . . . . .A
Prince . . . . .B
Principal . . . . . . .B
Principle . . . . . . .B
Prints . . . . .B
Prompt . . . . .A
Prop . . . . .A
Pry . . . . .A
Pug . . . . .A
Pump . . . . .A
Punch . . . . .A
Punt . . . . .A
Pupil . . . . .A
Purl . . . . .B
Purr . . . . .B
Putter . . . . .A

Q

Quack . . . . .A
Quarry . . . . .A
Queue . . . . .B
Quire . . . . .B
Quiver . . . . .A

R

Race . . . . .A
Rack . . . . .A
Racket . . . . .A
Raft . . . . .A
Rag . . . . .A
Rail . . . . .B
Rain . . . . .B
Raise . . . . .B
Rale . . . . .B
Rap . . . . . . .A & B
Rapper . . . . .B
Rapt . . . . .B
Rare . . . . .A
Rash . . . . .A
Rays . . . . .B
Raze . . . . .B
Read . . . . . . .B & C
Real . . . . .B
Ream . . . . .A
Rear . . . . .A
Rebel C
Record C
Red . . . . .B
Reed . . . . .B
Reel . . . . . . .A & B
Refrain . . . . .A
Refuse C
Reign . . . . .B

Rein . . . . .B
Rest . . . . .B
Retainer . . . . . . .A
Rhodes . . . . .B
Rhyme . . . . .B
Riddle . . . . .A
Rifle . . . . .A
Right . . . . .B
Ring . . . . .B
Ringer . . . . .A
Rime . . . . .B
Road . . . . .B
Roads . . . . .B
Rock . . . . .A
Rocky . . . . .A
Rode . . . . .B
Roe . . . . .B
Role . . . . .B
Roll . . . . .B
Roomer . . . . .B
Root . . . . .B
Rose . . . . .B
Rote . . . . .B
Rough . . . . .B
Route . . . . .B
Row . . . . . . .B & C
Rows . . . . .B
Rubber . . . . .A
Rude . . . . .B
Rued . . . . .B
Ruff . . . . .B
Ruler . . . . .A
Rumor . . . . .B
Rung . . . . .A
Rut . . . . .A
Rye . . . . .B

Group "A" (pp. 1–51)　　　Group "B" (pp. 53–106)　　　Group "C" (pp. 107–114)

S

Sack .... A	Sent .... B	Sloe .... B
Sage .... A	Serf .... B	Slow .... B
Sail .... B	Serial .... B	Slug .... A
Sale .... B	Set .... A	Smack .... A
Sake C	Sew .... B	Snake .... A
Sane .... B	Sewer ..... B & C	Snare .... A
Sap .... A	Shade .... A	Snarl .... A
Sash .... A	Sham .... A	So .... B
Saver .... B	Shear .... B	Soar .... B
Savor .... B	Shed .... A	Sock .... A
Saw .... A	Sheer .... B	Soil .... A
Scab .... A	Shoe .... B	Sole .... B
Scale .... A	Shone .... B	Solution .... A
Scent .... B	Shoo .... B	Some .... B
Score .... A	Shoot .... B	Son .... B
Scour .... A	Shore .... A	Sore .... B
Scout .... A	Shot .... A	Soul .... B
Scrap .... A	Shower ..... A & C	Sound .... A
Script .... A	Shown .... B	Sow .... B & C
Scrub .... A	Sic .... B	Spade ..... A & B
Scull .... B	Sick .... B	Spar .... A
Sea .... B	Sight .... B	Spayed .... B
Seal .... A	Singer C	Spell .... A
Sealer .... A	Sioux .... B	Spike .... A
Sealing .... B	Siren .... A	Spit .... A
Seam .... B	Site .... B	Spoke .... A
Seamen .... B	Size .... A	Spray .... A
Sedate .... A	Skate .... A	Spring .... A
See .... B	Skipper .... A	Spruce .... A
Seed .... B	Skull .... B	Squash .... A
Seem .... B	Slam .... A	Stable .... A
Seine .... B	Slaver C	Staff .... A
Sell .... B	Slay .... B	Stairs .... B
Seller .... B	Sleigh .... B	Stalk .... A
Semen .... B	Sleight .... B	Stall .... A
Sense .... B	Slew .... A	Stake .... B
	Slight .... B	Staple .... A
	Slip .... A	Stares .... B

Stationary . . . . . . .B	Sundae . . . . .B	Tender . . . . .A
Stationery . . . . . . .B	Sunday . . . . .B	Tense . . . . .B
Steak . . . . .B	Surf . . . . .B	Tents . . . . .B
Steal . . . . .B	Swallow . . . . . . .A	Terminal . . . . . . .A
Steel . . . . .B	Sweet . . . . .B	Tern . . . . .B
Steep . . . . .A	Symbol . . . . .B	Their . . . . .B
Steer . . . . .A		There . . . . .B
Stem . . . . .A	**T**	They're . . . . .B
Stern . . . . .A		Threw . . . . .B
Stew . . . . .A	Tab . . . . .A	Throne . . . . .B
Stick . . . . .A	Tack . . . . .A	Through . . . . . . .B
Stile . . . . .B	Tacked . . . . .B	Thrown . . . . . . .B
Still . . . . .A	Tacks . . . . .B	Tic . . . . .B
Stir . . . . .A	Tacky . . . . .A	Tick . . . . .B
Stole . . . . .A	Tact . . . . .B	Tide . . . . .B
Stoop . . . . .A	Tag . . . . .A	Tied . . . . .B
Store . . . . .A	Tail . . . . .B	Tier . . . . .B
Story . . . . .A	Tale . . . . .B	Till . . . . .A
Stout . . . . .A	Tan . . . . .A	Tiller . . . . .A
Straight . . . . .B	Tap . . . . .A	Timber . . . . .B
Strain . . . . .A	Taper . . . . .B	Timbre . . . . .B
Strait . . . . .B	Tapir . . . . .B	Tip . . . . .A
Strand . . . . .A	Tar . . . . .A	Tire . . . . .A
Straw . . . . .A	Tare . . . . .B	To . . . . .B
Strip . . . . .A	Tart . . . . .A	Toast . . . . .A
Stroke . . . . .A	Tattoo . . . . .A	Toll . . . . .A
Stud . . . . .A	Taught . . . . .B	Ton . . . . .B
Study . . . . .A	Taut . . . . .B	Too . . . . .B
Stunt . . . . .A	Tax . . . . .B	Top . . . . .A
Sty . . . . .A	Tea . . . . .B	Tower C
Style . . . . .B	Team . . . . .B	Train . . . . .A
Sub . . . . .A	Tear . . . . . .B & C	Tray . . . . .B
Subject C	Teas . . . . .B	Trey . . . . .B
Sue . . . . .B	Tease . . . . .B	Troll . . . . .A
Suer . . . . .B	Tee . . . . .B	Tun . . . . .B
Suite . . . . .B	Teem . . . . .B	Turn . . . . .B
Sum . . . . .B	Temple . . . . .A	Two . . . . .B
Sun . . . . .B	Tend . . . . .A	

U

Utter . . . . .A
Urn . . . . .B
Use C

V

Vain . . . . .B
Vale . . . . .B
Vamp . . . . .A
Vane . . . . .B
Vault . . . . .A
Veil . . . . .B
Vein . . . . .B
Vet . . . . .A
Vial . . . . .B
Vice . . . . .B
Vile . . . . .B
Vise . . . . .B
Volume . . . . .A

W

Waffle . . . . .A
Wage . . . . .A
Wail . . . . .B
Waist . . . . .B
Wait . . . . .B
Waive . . . . .B
Wake . . . . .A
Ware . . . . .B
Warn . . . . .B
Waste . . . . .B
Wave . . . . .B
Way . . . . .B
Weak . . . . .B
Wear . . . . .B

Week . . . . .B
Weigh . . . . .B
Weight . . . . .B
Well . . . . .A
Whale . . . . .B
Where . . . . .B
Whey . . . . .B
Whole . . . . .B
Wicked C
Will . . . . .A
Wind . . . . .B & C
Wined . . . . .B
Won . . . . .B
Wood . . . . .B
Worn . . . . .B
Would . . . . .B
Wound C
Wrap . . . . .B
Wrapped . . . . . . .B
Wrapper . . . . . . .B
Wright . . . . .B
Wring . . . . .B
Wrest . . . . .B
Wrote . . . . .B
Wry . . . . .B

XYZ

Yak . . . . .A
Yard . . . . .A
Yarn . . . . .A
Yen . . . . .A
Yew . . . . .B
Yoke . . . . .B
Yolk . . . . .B
You . . . . .B